Ripley's

Believe It or Not!

Developed and produced by Ripley Publishing Ltd

This edition published and distributed by:

Mason Crest
450 Parkway Drive, Suite D, Broomall, PA 19008
www.masoncrest.com

Printed and bound in the United States of America

First printing
9 8 7 6 5 4 3 2 1

Ripley's Believe It or Not!
That's Weird!
ISBN: 978-1-4222-3153-1 (hardback)
Ripley's Believe It or Not!—Complete 8 Title Series
ISBN: 978-1-4222-3147-0

Cataloging-in-Publication Data on file with the Library of Congress

PUBLISHER'S NOTE
While every effort has been made to verify the accuracy of the entries in this book, the
Publishers cannot be held responsible for any errors contained in the work. They would
be glad to receive any information from readers.

WARNING
Some of the stunts and activities in this book are undertaken by experts and should not
be attempted by anyone without adequate training and supervision.

Ripley's Believe It or Not!

Download The Weird

THAT'S WEIRD!

www.MasonCrest.com

THATS WEIRD!

Crazy tales. Enter into a world of strange
stories. Read about the house that doubles
up as a hangar, the very messy World
Custard Pie Throwing Championships,
and the dress made of cheese!

The Maeklong Market Railway in Thailand
runs through the market, forcing vendors
to move when a train passes through...

Inflated Extras

Next time you see a big scene in a Hollywood movie, look a little closer at the people in the background, for they might not be quite as they appear. You might expect a little computer-generated magic, but perhaps not thousands of individually inflated latex dummies.

The Inflatable Crowd Company, started by Joe Biggins in 2002, provides hordes of rubber dummies to the movie industry, dressed to look like real crowds on screen. Joe's dummies have been fallen soldiers in the Battle of Iwo Jima in World War II (*Flags of Our Fathers*, 2006), victims of a deadly virus outbreak (*Contagion*, 2011), 11,000 fans at a 1930s boxing match (*Cinderella Man*, 2005), and a 7,000-strong horse-racing crowd (*Seabiscuit*, 2003).

Joe was working on the movie *Seabiscuit* when he was asked how to fill the grandstands for the horse-racing scenes in an authentic but economical way. After testing cardboard cutouts, which were the usual method, he realized that the fake figures needed to be portable and three-dimensional. He considered the idea of inflatables, but found that nobody in the industry had done this before so there were none available. He created a prototype torso designed to sit in a stadium and the film's director, Gary Ross, agreed to use 7,000 such inflatables for *Seabiscuit*. Joe started his company after filming had ended.

One year later, there was such demand for the inflatable bodies that Joe and his business partner Richard McIntosh had increased their stock to 30,000 pump-up extras, complete with clothing, masks, and wigs.

inflatable actors!

The first full-bodied inflatables were created for *Flags of Our Fathers* (2006) to act as fallen soldiers at the Battle of Iwo Jima, shot in Iceland. The bodies were modified according to the scene—some were filled with plaster to emulate the reaction of a solid body when it is run over by a tank. Water corpses were also made, weighted to float or sink the way a human body would. In 2006, police were called when a body was found at the bottom of a waterfall in Iceland; rescue teams and a helicopter were deployed, but what they discovered was an escaped member of the Inflatable Crowd Company.

DID YOU SPOT THE THOUSANDS OF DUMMIES USED IN THESE FAMOUS FILMS?

CINDERELLA MAN (2005)	11,000
FRIDAY NIGHT LIGHTS (2004)	8,000
WIMBLEDON (2004)	7,000
SEABISCUIT (2003)	7,000
MILLION DOLLAR BABY (2004)	3,000
WE ARE MARSHALL (2006)	2,400
IRON MAN 2 (2010)	2,100
THE FIGHTER (2010)	1,800
THE DAMNED UNITED (2009)	1,800
THE KING'S SPEECH (2010)	1,500
AMERICAN GANGSTER (2007)	1,500
SPIDER-MAN 3 (2007)	1,000
ALVIN AND THE CHIPMUNKS 2 (2009)	550
SALT (2010)	500
CONTAGION (2011)	200
FROST/NIXON (2008)	100

BEHIND THE SCENES

From a distance, the dummies look so genuine when they are fitted with diverse masks and costumes that thousands can be used for one scene, and film producers don't have to hire real-life extras. Each crowd member must be inflated, dressed, and placed on their seat, and fitted with individual wigs and masks. At the end of filming they all need to be deflated, packed, and shipped to another film or back to storage. Outdoor filming presents the biggest problems. When filming on a beach in Iceland for *Flags of Our Fathers*, the dummies were nearly blown into the sea by strong winds. When the clothed inflatables are soaked from rain, they are twice as heavy. Real-life actors are usually placed in the foreground and randomly throughout the rubber crowd. As the human extras move, they create the illusion of a teeming mass in the background of the scene. The dolls have also been used for commercials, TV shows, and music videos.

The Inflatable Crowd Company supplied 200 corpses for a mass grave filmed for *Contagion* (2011).

A boxing scene in *American Gangster* (2007) starring Denzel Washington. If you look closely, the dummies can be seen sitting to the left and right of some of the real-life extras. Fifteen hundred dummies were inflated for the scene.

A rubber crowd looks on during filming for the college football movie *We Are Marshall* (2006). Two thousand four hundred dummies were used. The only real people in the crowd were seen walking up the stadium steps.

Food Covers

A Japanese company has designed a range of iPhone covers that look like food. The plastic cases mimic such dishes as sushi rolls, chocolate desserts, and bacon and eggs.

🄡 **VIDEO SPOOFS** Corey Vidal of Oakville, Canada, makes a living from posting videos on YouTube. He specializes in pop culture spoofs and light-hearted instructional videos, and in just four years his videos have been seen more than 50 million times. "YouTube saved my life," he says.

🄡 **YOUNG DESIGNER** At just 13 years of age, Aaron Bond from Devon, England, has designed and produced an iPhone app video game. Aaron, who set up his own web company when he was only six years old, learned how to write a smartphone game by watching online tutorials. The game, "Spud Run," involves navigating a mutant potato through a maze before it is mashed.

🄡 **CUTEST DOG** After his U.S. owner posted pictures of him on Facebook, Boo, a five-year-old Pomeranian dog, has amassed more than two million "likes," landed a book deal, and been named the cutest dog in the world. He acquired the look of a cuddly teddy bear by accident, his natural long hair having become so knotted it had to be shaved off.

🄡 **AIR PHONE** An iPhone app has been designed that blows out air through the phone's speakers. It is powerful enough to extinguish the candles on a birthday cake.

🄡 **SPEED RECORD** On August 22, 2010, Melissa Thompson from Manchester, England, wrote the text message "the razor-toothed piranhas of the genera Serrasalmus and Pygocentrus are the most ferocious freshwater fish in the world. In reality they seldom attack a human" in a record time of 25.94 seconds.

NINTENDO WAS FOUNDED IN 1889—IT STARTED BY MAKING PLAYING CARDS.

🄡 **SMELLY PHONE** The Japanese-produced F-022 cell phone has a detachable fragrance chip that owners can saturate with perfume, which then infuses the entire phone with the chosen scent.

🄡 **GREAT CATCH** A YouTube clip showed a spectator at a 2011 baseball game between the Toronto Blue Jays and the Kansas City Royals catching a foul ball—in his popcorn bucket.

🄡 **FAST FLIGHT** U.S. photographer Nate Bolt posted a video on YouTube showing a flight from San Francisco to Paris, France, in just 124 seconds. Armed with a camera and a time-lapse controller, he took a picture approximately every 20–30 seconds of the 11-hour journey from take-off to landing, a total of 2,459 shots.

🄡 **EXPERT DANCER** On August 29, 2010, nine-year-old Ryota Wada from Herndon, Virginia, became the youngest person to achieve a perfect score on the expert level of the video game "Dance Dance Revolution." He mastered all 223 steps and 16 combinations while dancing to the song "Heavy Eurobeat."

🄡 **BAD MAPS** In November 2010, a Nicaraguan military commander blamed faulty Google maps for an accidental incursion by Nicaraguan soldiers into Costa Rica.

Paul Silviak's head and Robert Mahler's body make up this horsemaning pose with a guillotine, taken by Brent Douglas in Oregon.

Jeffrey Bautista and Paul Riddle from San Jose, California, horsemaning in formalwear.

facebook fad

Los Angeles photographer Deney Tuazon took this shot featuring Jade Zivalic's head and Isaiah Castellanos' body in San Francisco.

In the Facebook fad of horsemaning, two people pose for prank pictures to make it look as if one of them has lost their head. The craze for posing for photos as headless horsemen (hence the name) was actually around in the 1920s—long before the advent of the Internet.

SUCKED INTO PIPE Writer Allan Baillie of Sydney, Australia, survived with just cuts and bruises after being sucked feet-first into a drainage pipe and spat out onto a nearby beach seconds later. He was swimming in a pool while a workman was cleaning it, and when the workman pressed the button to open the water valve, Baillie was sucked into the pipe. The circumference of the pipe was smaller than his body, but luckily the tremendous pressure meant that he popped straight out at the other end like a wine cork.

STEADY HAND Performing in Hamburg in 2010, German stuntman Joe Alexander used his elbow to break a record 24 concrete blocks, assembled in three stacks of eight, demonstrating such skill that the egg he was holding in his smashing hand did not break.

HUMAN BLOCKHEADS At the ninth annual Sideshow Gathering at Wilkes-Barre, Pennsylvania, in November 2010, 36 people simultaneously hammered various objects into their noses to create a mass human blockhead.

JUNIOR TEACHER Shruti Pandey was just four years old when she began teaching yoga to adults at a retreat in Uttar Pradesh, India. Her elder brother, Harsh Kumar, had learned all 84 yoga positions by the age of five.

DEXTROUS TOES After losing both of his hands at age three in an accident with electricity lines in his native China, Luo Yanbo has learned to eat, write, and brush his teeth with his feet. His grandmother taught him how to use chopsticks with his feet and he has become so adept that he can even use his toes to make phone calls.

FOREIGN ACCENT When Karen Butler of Toledo, Oregon, went for dental surgery to remove several teeth, she came round from the anesthetic with a British accent—even though she has never traveled to Europe or lived outside the United States. She suffers from foreign accent syndrome, a rare neurological disorder caused by an injury to the part of the brain that controls speech. There have been only about 100 known cases since the condition was first reported in the 1940s.

RAISED ARM Sadhu Amar Bharati Urdhavaahu, an Indian holy man, has kept his right arm raised above his head continuously for decades as a sign of his devotion.

THE STRANGE CAREER OF ELMER McCURDY'S CORPSE

Inept at robbing trains, Oklahoma outlaw Elmer McCurdy made more in death than he ever did while he was alive. He was killed in a 1911 gunfight, his last words being the familiar "You'll never take me alive," but it was then that his corpse took on a life of its own. When nobody came forward to claim it, the undertaker had it embalmed with a preservative and exhibited as *The Bandit Who Wouldn't Give Up* with customers inserting a nickel in McCurdy's mouth. The attraction proved so profitable that numerous carnival operators put in bids for the dead outlaw, but the undertaker resisted all offers until being duped by a man claiming to be McCurdy's brother. Led to believe that McCurdy was to be given a proper burial, the undertaker handed him over, only to see him exhibited in a traveling carnival two weeks later.

For the next 60 years, McCurdy's body was sold to various wax museums and carnivals, although one haunted house owner in South Dakota turned it down because he did not think it was sufficiently lifelike. Then in 1976, during the filming of an episode of the TV series *The Six Million Dollar Man* at the Californian amusement park known as "The Pike," a crew member moved what he thought was a mannequin hanging from a gallows and got the shock of his life when the arm fell off to reveal mummified human remains. It was Elmer McCurdy. The following year, Elmer was finally buried in Oklahoma, the state medical examiner ordering that his casket be buried in concrete so that his corpse would never be disturbed again.

SUMO SPLITS Although Matt Alaeddine from Edmonton, Canada, weighs more than 400 lb (180 kg), he is a contortionist. Despite his considerable bulk, he can press the soles of his feet to the cheeks of his face by doing the "sumo splits."

BIKER IMPALED During a motorcycle accident in January 2011, a 20-year-old man in Delhi, India, was impaled through his chest by inch-thick (2.5-cm) iron rods. Doctors saved his life in a four-hour operation.

ASHES TATTOO Brother and sister Andrew and Helen Bird of Stoke-on-Trent, England, created a lasting tribute to their dead grandfather by having his ashes tattooed into their skin. Andrew had an extract from one of grandpa Reginald Alefs' poems etched on to his arm while Helen had a rose inked onto her back. The tattoo artist mixed some of Mr. Alefs' ashes with ink to create the artworks.

INTERNAL DECAPITATION The impact of a car accident jolted two-year-old Micah Andrews' head sideways with such force that his skull separated from his spine—a condition called atlanto-occipital dislocation, or internal decapitation. Surgeons in Phoenix, Arizona, kept Micah's head still by placing sandbags on either side before implanting a titanium loop to reattach the base of the skull to the spine. The rod is held in place with a piece of the boy's rib. Two months later, Micah was released from hospital, able to walk and talk again.

GIANT TUMOR A massive tumor, accounting for one-third of his body weight, was removed from the back of a Chinese teenager in 2011. The 41-lb (19-kg) growth had been expanding on the body of 15-year-old Qiu Sheng, from Yunnan Province, since birth. It started as two bean-sized tumors on his waist, before growing first to the size of a peach, then a coconut, and finally a sandbag on his back that grew into his chest cavity and pushed aside his right shoulder blade.

RUSTY BULLET In 2011, doctors finally discovered why a Chinese farmer had been affected by epilepsy for more than two decades—a ¾-in-long (2-cm) rusty bullet had been lodged in his brain since 1988. Wang Tianqing of Zhangjiakou City remembered being knocked unconscious by a blow to the head, but had no idea he had been shot.

PLAYING TWISTER Chen Daorong from Zhengzhou, Fujian Province, China, at age 80 years is a contortionist. He started contorting his body in 1999 to cure back pains and is now so supple that he can twist his legs around his neck, do the splits, and sleep resting his head on one foot, as a pillow.

NASTY SHOCK Joseph Ferrato of Akron, Ohio, sustained only minor injuries after 23,000 volts of electricity burst through the windshield of his car. The damage was caused by a falling power line that had been cut down by copper thieves.

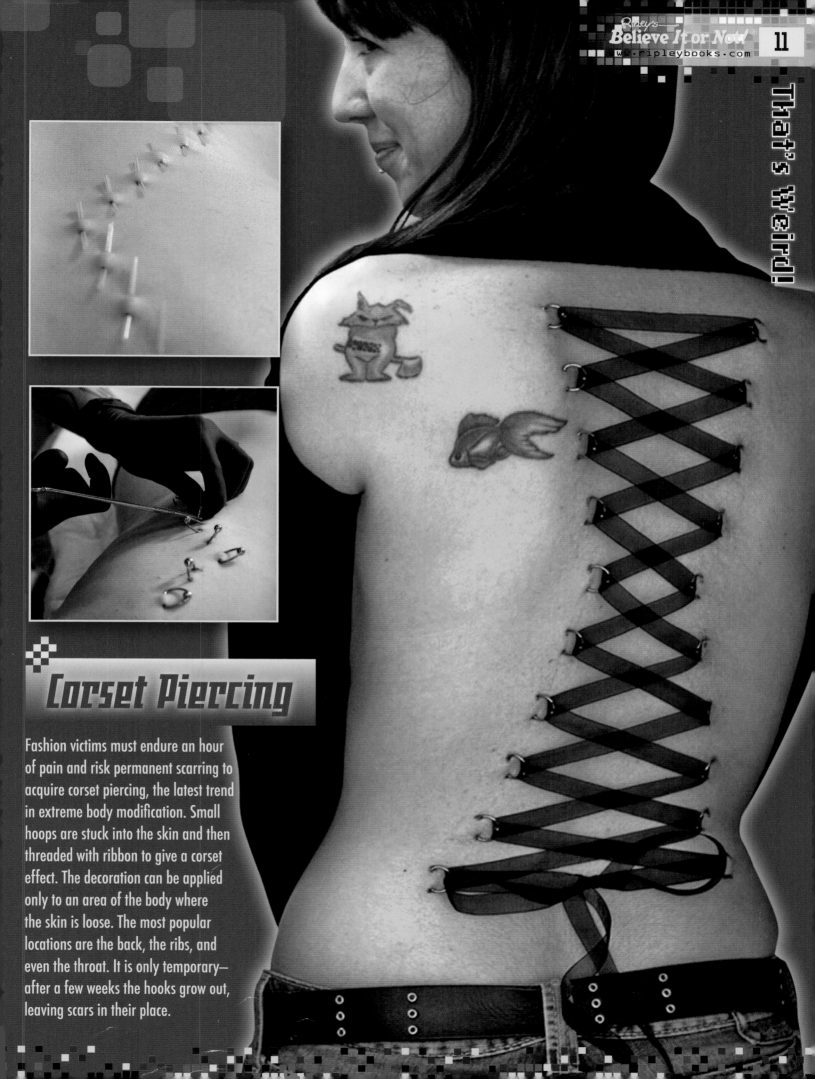

Corset Piercing

Fashion victims must endure an hour of pain and risk permanent scarring to acquire corset piercing, the latest trend in extreme body modification. Small hoops are stuck into the skin and then threaded with ribbon to give a corset effect. The decoration can be applied only to an area of the body where the skin is loose. The most popular locations are the back, the ribs, and even the throat. It is only temporary—after a few weeks the hooks grow out, leaving scars in their place.

MARKET RAILWAY

The Maeklong Market Railway in Thailand runs right through the heart of the market, forcing the vendors to pull back their awnings and move their produce out of the way when the train comes along. Passing just inches from the vendors' faces, the train ruthlessly crushes any stray fruit or vegetables left in its path.

■ HIGH SPEED A Chinese passenger train traveling between Beijing and Shanghai can reach the incredible speed of 302 mph (486 km/h). The new high-speed train has halved travel times between the two cities from ten hours to five.

■ CROWDED TRAINS India's rail system serves about six billion passengers every year—that's nearly equal to the entire population of the Earth.

■ PIPE DREAM Anthony Smith, an 85-year-old grandfather from London, England, crossed the Atlantic Ocean in 2011 on a 40-ft-long (12-m) raft that was made from lengths of gas and water pipes. He and his three-man crew—all of whom were aged over 55—set sail from the Canary Islands for the 66-day, 2,800-mi (4,506-km) voyage to the Caribbean.

■ RECYCLED BOAT Taiwan's Alex Chou designed an eco boat made primarily from 700 plastic bottles. The sailboat *Forever*, built entirely from recycled materials and powered by wind and solar energy, made its maiden voyage in June 2011.

■ RESCUE MISSION After spending nine years building a two-seater airplane in the basement of his home in Lower Allen Township, Pennsylvania, Dan Reeves realized it was too big to get up the steps. So he dug a trench down to the foundation, knocked out a wall and, with the help of neighbors, used a heavy chain to pull the plane up into daylight.

SINKING FEELING

Love, Love, a boat created by French artist Julien Berthier, floats at a constant 45-degree angle to give the impression that it is sinking. Berthier split an abandoned 21-ft-long (6.5-m) yacht, sealed it with fiberglass, repositioned the keel, built a new seat, and put two electrical motors underneath the vessel to power it. The effect is so convincing that when the boat appeared on Lake Constance, Germany, dozens of people called the harbormasters to tell them a boat was sinking.

SHOE CAR A Chinese shoe manufacturer has converted a giant shoe into an electric car. The 10-ft-long (3-m), 3-ft-high (90-cm) shoe car has leather bodywork and took six months to create from the hide of five bulls. It can carry two people 250 mi (400 km) at a top speed of 20 mph (32 km/h) on a single charge of the battery, which is located beneath the driver's seat in the heel.

DRY RUN Battling against extreme heat and sandstorms, Reza Pakravan from London, England, cycled 1,084 mi (1,734 km) across the Sahara Desert in 13 days 5 hours, averaging more than 80 mi (130 km) a day. The heat was so fierce that he had to drink around 15 pt (7 l) of water every day to keep hydrated.

ELECTRIC TRIKE Four engineers from Hamburg, Germany, have devised a tricycle powered solely by two 18-volt electric screwdrivers. The 44-lb (20-kg) EX trike, which can reach speeds of 18.6 mph (30 km/h), is driven in a headlong position, the driver operating the brake and gas levers with his hands and the rear wheel with his legs.

$1-MILLION CRASH A woman driver in Monte Carlo caused a $1-million car accident in July 2011 by crashing into some of the most expensive cars in the world as she tried to negotiate her way around the famous Place du Casino. Her $375,000 Bentley Azure scraped the side of a $110,000 Mercedes before hitting a $200,000 Ferrari, a $225,000 Aston Martin Rapide, and a $120,000 Porsche 911.

BUS PROPOSAL Romantic British bus driver Phill Openshaw used the digital display on the front of his vehicle to propose to his girlfriend Sam Woodward. He changed the electronic board on his Wilts and Dorset bus to read: "Sam, Will you marry me?" She was waiting at a bus stop in the town of Poole when she saw the sign—and said yes!

Tricky Trike

A man in Jaipur, India, was seen transporting the chassis of an old car attached to the frame of his tricycle. He pushed his trike with his head through the open hood of the car so that he could see where he was going.

EXPLODING MANHOLE An exploding manhole caused by flash floods threw an unoccupied parked car several feet into the air in Montreal, Quebec, Canada, in July 2011. The torrent of water turned the manhole into a geyser which tossed the rear half of the vehicle repeatedly into the air.

Man Jumps Speeding **Lamborghini**

Videos showing Alassan Issa Gobitaca jumping from a standing start over sports cars traveling at up to 60 mph (97 km/h) have amazed millions of viewers online. To date, Alassan has cleared every speeding car that has driven at him, and the Swedish daredevil has ambitions to leap over even faster cars, perhaps two at once.

R **MASCOT BRAWL** The Duck, mascot of the University of Oregon football team, received a one-game suspension after being involved in a brawl with Shasta the cougar, mascot of the University of Houston. The 20-second YouTube video shows the Duck laying into his opposite number with fists and webbed feet.

R **VIDEO PROPOSAL** Matt Still proposed to his unsuspecting girlfriend Ginny Joiner via the giant screen at a movie theater in Atlanta, Georgia—and the video of his elaborate marriage proposal racked up over 20 million hits on YouTube in its first four months online. Ginny had gone to the theater with her brother expecting to see the action–adventure movie *Fast Five*, when her boyfriend's video suddenly appeared on screen after the trailers had finished. When Matt's mini-movie was over, he appeared for real in the movie theater to place the ring on stunned Ginny's finger.

R **CHICK RESCUE** A visitor to Ireland's Dublin Zoo uploaded a clip to YouTube showing a 210-lb (95-kg) orangutan tenderly rescuing a drowning chick by lifting it from the water using a leaf. Seeing the tiny moorhen chick struggling in the pond of his enclosure, Jorong, a Bornean orangutan, pulled a leaf from a nearby bush and held it out for the bird to cling to. At the second attempt, he managed to save the chick, then placed it down on the grass and stroked its head.

R **FLATTENED SNOWMAN** A bus driver lost his job after his bosses saw a YouTube video of him running over a snowman that had been built in the road at Urbana, Illinois.

R **DOG BITES SHARK** A video clip of a dog biting a shark in the ocean near Broome, Western Australia, has been viewed 4.5 million times on YouTube. Two dogs were swimming in the sea and appeared to be herding several sharks toward shore, when one suddenly ducked under the water and attacked a shark before emerging unscathed.

R **POPULAR AD** As of March 2012, Evian's "Roller-Skating Babies" ad had been watched over 105 million times via video websites, making it the world's most viewed online advertisement.

Break-dancing **Gorilla**

Millions of people have watched this clip of Zola the gorilla dancing at a zoo in Canada. Zola's keepers at the zoo told Ripley's about the video: "Zola, the Calgary Zoo's nine-year-old gorilla is seen here in a shifting area of his enclosure having some playtime in a puddle of water. The keeper was able to capture the action on video and when music was added to the clip, Zola appears to have quite the moves! Western Lowland gorillas are critically endangered and hopefully this bit of video fun can raise awareness of this and of the importance of captive breeding programs. Zola came to the Calgary Zoo three years ago from the Bronx Zoo."

HUMAN CLOUD A video clip of a cloud formation in Canada that appears to show the face of a Roman god notched up over 300,000 hits on YouTube in just four days. The cloud, shaped in a humanlike side profile complete with mouth, nose, and eyes, was filmed as a storm gathered over Grand Falls, New Brunswick.

BROOM ROUTINE Beijing road sweeper Zhang Xiufang became a Chinese TV celebrity after performing tai chi in the street using her broom as an exercise prop to keep in shape. A passerby filmed a short video of her routine on his mobile phone and posted it online, where it was such a hit that she was invited to star on a national TV show.

CHEATED DEATH A YouTube clip taken from his helmet camera as he plunged to the ground shows skydiver Michael Holmes somehow surviving a 15,000-ft (4,573-m) fall after both his parachute and reserve chute failed to open on a jump in New Zealand. He escaped with just two broken bones and some bruising.

Jenny the Pug

Jenny the Pug from Portland, Oregon, became a YouTube celebrity after videos of her pushing her puppy stroller around her hometown gained a huge online audience. Probably the most famous pug in the world, Jenny has even made an appearance on *The Tonight Show* with Jay Leno.

David After Dentist

In 2008, David DeVore from Lake Mary, Florida, made a video of his seven-year-old son, David, under the effects of anesthetic after a dental procedure, which had a bizarre effect on his behavior. When David Snr. uploaded the footage to YouTube in January 2009, he was expecting only family and friends to watch it, but the clip has since become a global phenomenon, attracting more than 100 million views, musical remixes, and tribute videos. You can even buy T-shirts and stickers printed with David's drowsy "Is This Real Life?" catchphrase. In the picture, top right, David models one of his T-shirts.

LEAPING SHARK An amazing video of a shark jumping over a surfer off New Smyrna Beach, Florida, became an online hit in 2011. Photographer Jacob Langston captured the spinner shark's daring leap while he was filming surfers for the *Orlando Sentinel* newspaper.

HEAD TURNER A YouTube clip shows a Russian waiter named Alexander turning his head and neck 180 degrees to look behind him. It was during gymnastics training that he first realized he had a spinal abnormality, which made his body extremely flexible. He says he has to concentrate energy from his whole body to perform the feat.

APPLES ARE 25% AIR, WHICH IS WHY THEY FLOAT.

TWINS RESTAURANT New York City's Twins Restaurant is owned by identical twin sisters Lisa and Debbie Ganz and is staffed by 37 sets of identical twins who work the same shift in the same uniform. Even the restaurant's business cards, doorknobs, light fittings, mirrors, and bar stools are doubles.

PRISON BAKERY A team of 20 convicts at Rikers Island prison in New York bake 36,000 loaves of bread a week—enough to feed the prison's population of 13,000. The prison bakery covers an area of 11,000 sq ft (1,020 sq m).

ROYAL BEAN When Wesley Hosie of Somerset, England, found a mango-flavored jelly bean bearing what looked like an image of Kate Middleton, Duchess of Cambridge—complete with long hair and smile—he put it up for sale on eBay at a price of £515.

PINEAPPLE PAINKILLER Pineapple is a natural painkiller. The fruit contains enzymes that can reduce the inflammation associated with arthritis and in this way bring pain relief.

STUFFED SHIRT On the U.S. TV show *Late Night with Jimmy Fallon* on March 1, 2011, George Booth stuffed a record 185 hot dogs into his T-shirt in 30 seconds.

CHEESE PLATTER A cheese platter weighing 2,475 lb (1,125 kg) was placed on show at the World Cheese Awards in Birmingham, England. The platter consisted of 139 different wedges, featuring cheeses from every country in Europe as well as from the Americas, Australasia, and Africa.

SUPER SUSHI A restaurant in Aichi Prefecture, Japan, serves giant sushi rolls that are wrapped in 6 ft 6 in (2 m) of seaweed and rice. The rolls, which contain 20 foods and cost just under $200, must be preordered two days in advance.

Foodie Fashion

A model shows off a dress made of nori seaweed with a dead octopus necklace at a fashion food exhibition in Berlin, Germany. After appearing on the catwalk, the designs were eaten. Other outfits included a chocolate dress with a quails' egg necklace and a bacon suit topped with a salad headdress.

CUPCAKE KING Competitive eater Tim "Eater X" Janus from New York City ate a record 42 cupcakes in 8 minutes at the Isle Waterloo World Cupcake Eating Championship on April 23, 2011. He has also eaten 141 pieces of nigiri sushi in 6 minutes, nearly 12 lb (5.4 kg) of burritos in 10 minutes, and 7 lb 11 oz (3.5 kg) of boneless buffalo wings in 12 minutes.

ROYAL REBUFF In August 2011, the King and Queen of Sweden were turned away by a German restaurant owner who failed to recognize them. King Carl XVI Gustaf and Queen Silvia called at a 16th-century inn in Ladenburg, but proprietor Nadine Schellenberger was preoccupied with a wedding reception and told them there was no table available. The royal couple and their entourage instead went out for a pizza on the market square.

MINI BAR As part of a campaign to save their local pub, The Plough, residents of Shepreth in Cambridgeshire, England, opened up a village telephone box to serve beer. The Dog and Bone was open for only one night, but in that time it served about 70 customers.

FULLY BOOKED A wall in Brushstroke, a Japanese restaurant in New York City, is made from 12,000 old paperback books.

BOILED EGGS While on board the U.S.S. *Fitzgerald* on August 13, 2011, Adrian Morgan of Baton Rouge, Louisiana, ate 20 hard-boiled eggs in 84 seconds—one every four seconds.

BEAN BARMY Although baked beans originated in the United States, the British are such fans of the food that each year they eat more than 800 million cans—three times more than the rest of the world combined.

SPAM SANDWICH An open sandwich weighing 1,652 lb (750 kg)—including about 1,400 lb (635 kg) of Spam—was produced in Fremont, Nebraska, in 2011.

HIGH TEA In Los Angeles, California, a giant tea bag made from cheesecloth was unveiled measuring 6 x 4 ft (1.8 x 1.2 m) and weighing 151 lb (68.5 kg).

® DOUGHNUT DELIVERY In 2011, Voodoo Doughnuts of Portland, Oregon, made a record-breaking box of doughnuts, weighing 666 lb (302 kg), measuring 7 x 7 x 5 ft (2 x 2 x 1.5 m), and filled with about 3,880 doughnuts.

® GIANT BURGER A hamburger and bun grilled at the 2011 Alameda County Fair, California, by Brett Enright and Nick Nicora, weighed a staggering 777 lb (352 kg). It took 13 hours to cook and measured 5 ft (1.5 m) in diameter, and was 3 ft (90 cm) thick, representing a whole cow's worth of beef. The cheese on top of the burger weighed 50 lb (22.7 kg), and was accompanied by 30 lb (13.6 kg) of lettuce, 20 lb (9 kg) of onions, 12 lb (5.4 kg) of pickles, 10 lb (4.5 kg) of mustard, and 10 lb (4.5 kg) of ketchup. The bun, which took six hours to bake, weighed 272 lb (123 kg) and was 28 in (70 cm) thick.

® DREAM CARS The interior of a restaurant in Surabaya, Indonesia, allows customers to eat in converted classic cars. Dream Cars features a 1949 Mercedes Benz limo that has been modified into a dining table that seats 20 people, and a 1962 Chevrolet Impala, which has been transformed into a smaller table for four. A 1961 brown Cadillac forms a seating area, a 1959 yellow Lotus houses an organ and the restaurant's audio system, while a 1969 red Chevrolet Corvette has been converted into an aquarium holding 100 fish.

® FISHY TASTE Japanese scientists who conducted tests to determine why red wine should not be drunk with fish found that the greater amount of iron there is in a wine, the more likely it is to leave a fishy aftertaste when consumed with seafood.

® FAST FOOD McDonald's restaurants feed more than 64 million people a day—more than the entire population of the U.K.

® BIRTHDAY BASH On September 1, 2011, a 48.6-gal (184-l) bottle of Jack Daniel's Tennessee Whiskey was produced to celebrate what would have been Jack Daniel's 161st birthday. A bottle orchestra played "Happy Birthday" on 475 bottles of Jack Daniel's while fans of the liquor sent Jack a digital birthday card containing 1,075 individual greetings.

® DOUGHNUT BURGER The 2011 New York State Fair at Syracuse unveiled the 1,500-calorie Big Kahuna Donut Burger—a quarter-pound burger, with cheese, bacon, lettuce, tomato, and onion, in between slices of doughnut.

CUSTARD CHAOS!

Competitors from as far away as Canada, Japan, South Africa, and Germany travel to Kent, England, to take part in the annual World Custard Pie Throwing Championships. Points are awarded for throwing pies squarely into opponents' faces and also for the most amusing and original throwing techniques. The event was first held in 1967 and was inspired by a Charlie Chaplin comedy movie.

WORLD CUSTARD PIE TROPHY

WACKY WEBSITES

Don't like tomatoes? There is a site dedicated to the belief that tomatoes are evil and cannot be trusted.

Loaf of bread cam allows you to watch a loaf of bread slowly going stale.

A toilet paper site enables you to unroll toilet paper for as long as you want without having to wind it up again.

The Iowa State University **Entomology Club website** offers a selection of tasty insect recipes.

A dancing cows website shows cows doing ballet, disco, and other dances.

Like repetition? Try the site that lets you open doors over and over again.

Would your **cat look good in a wig?** Visit the site catering for all your kitty wig needs.

The University of Virginia has a site that helps you **dissect a frog online**.

If you like watching paint dry, you might also like the site that enables you to **watch paint peel**.

Check out the site that helps you to find **prison pen pals**.

The University of Oklahoma Police Department website has a **Citizen's Self-Arrest Form** that lets you hand yourself over to the cops.

Does your cat look like Hitler? Check out the site that shows pictures of cats that resemble the Nazi leader.

GOING, GOING, GONE!
(weird items sold on eBay)

- Ian Usher of Perth, Australia, sold his entire life for $380,000. The sale price included his home, his car, his motorcycle, a two-week trial in his job, and even his friends.

- Mary Anderson of Indiana put her dead husband's metal walking cane up for sale because his ghost was said to be haunting the house and scaring her grandson. It fetched $65,000.

- A ten-year-old half-eaten grilled cheese sandwich bearing a likeness of the Virgin Mary was bought for $28,000.

- When Melissa Heuschkel from Connecticut couldn't decide what to name her fourth child, she put the rights up for sale on eBay. Online casino Golden Palace paid $15,100 to name the baby Golden Palace Benedetto.

- The right to push a button detonating an explosion to demolish a building in Charleston, West Virginia, sold for $5,207.

- Justin Timberlake's half-eaten French toast (complete with fork and syrup) sold for $3,154.

10 MAJOR TWITTER RUSHES
(number of tweets per second)

August 28, 2011, Beyoncé announces her pregnancy at MTV Video Music Awards 8,868

July 17, 2011, Women's World Cup final (soccer), U.S. v. Japan 7,196

July 17, 2011, Copa America (soccer), Paraguay v. Brazil 7,166

January 1, 2011, New Year's Day, Japan 6,939

June 26, 2011, B.E.T. (Black Entertainment Television) Awards 6,436

May 28, 2011, UEFA Champions League final (soccer), Manchester United v. Barcelona 6,303

June 12, 2011, NBA finals, Dallas Mavericks v. Miami Heat 5,531

March 11, 2011, Japanese earthquake 5,530

August 23, 2011, Washington, D.C. earthquake 5,449

That's Weird!

- A bucket of manure from Britain's 2004 Olympic gold-medal-winning horse Shear L'Eau fetched $1,392.
- A cheesy Dorito in the shape of the Pope's miter sold for $1,209.
- A pair of singer Bryan Adams's dirty socks sold for $750.
- A plastic fern from Elvis Presley's Graceland home sold for $600.
- Collected from a London hotel, a piece of Britney Spears' used chewing gum sold for $263.
- Three snowballs taken from blizzards that submerged the Loveland, Colorado, house of Jim and Mary Walker sold for $200.
- A UFO enthusiast paid $135 for a UFO detector said to be able to recognize foreign objects in the sky.
- A supposedly haunted rubber duck was snapped up for $107.50.
- A bottle of air from England's Lake District—described as "the perfect accompaniment" to the culture of poet William Wordsworth—was bought for $90.
- A potato in the shape of Mickey Mouse sold for $7.50.

- A 19th-century vampire hunting kit—including a hammer, four stakes, a prayer book, and a crucifix—fetched $2,005.50.

STRANGEST APPS

- ○ Throw a virtual pie at someone you have a photo of.
- ○ Blow air out of your phone's speaker to snuff out the candles on your birthday cake.
- ○ Convert your phone into a working metal detector.
- ○ Immortalize yourself as a butter sculpture.
- ○ Pop virtual bubble wrap.
- ○ Receive regular messages from an imaginary girlfriend.
- ○ Detect the ripeness of a watermelon.
- ○ Transform your cell phone into a virtual fart machine.
- ○ Play a collection of 16 annoying noises to put your teeth on edge, including a jackhammer, a baby crying, and a chainsaw.
- ○ Drink a virtual beer.
- ○ Whistle to call your dog.
- ○ Calculate your time and cause of death on the Death Time Calculator.
- ○ Read about weird genetic diseases.
- ○ Play a trombone.

7 FASCINATING FACEBOOK FACTS

- Al Pacino's face was on the original Facebook homepage.
- One in every 8.3 people on Earth is on Facebook.
- Over 60 percent of people use Facebook to find out how ex-partners are doing.
- The average user on Facebook has 190 friends.
- A Facebook employee hoodie sold for $4,000 on eBay.
- There is a medical condition called Facebook Addiction Disorder.
- John Watson of New York City was reunited with the long-lost daughter he had been seeking for 20 years after finding her Facebook profile.

A Cut Above

International pop star Lady Gaga is renowned for outrageous style, designed by her own Haus of Gaga fashion house, but nothing has come close to the genuine meat dress she sported at the 2010 MTV Video Music Awards in Los Angeles. The layered beefsteak number, complete with a meat hat, was designed by Franc Fernandez and Haus of Gaga. The dress was saved from being eaten by the Rock and Roll Hall of Fame in Cleveland, Ohio.

Unbelievable GAGA

In 2010, *Time* magazine compiled a list of the 100 most influential people in the world, based on Twitter and Facebook. Lady Gaga came second, beaten only by President Obama.

By September 2013, Lady Gaga had gathered a remarkable 39.2 million Twitter followers—that's three times the population of Ireland—making her the most popular "tweeter" in the world.

In 2009, Lady Gaga spent over $1,000 on pizza for fans waiting at an autograph signing in Los Angeles.

The 2011 single *Born This Way* achieved one million iTunes downloads in just five days, becoming the fastest ever million-selling song on the iTunes store.

Lady Gaga's YouTube music video *Bad Romance* has been viewed more than 569 million times. That's over 1.5 views for every American.

Did you know? Lady Gaga went to high school with Paris Hilton in Manhattan, New York.

The University of South Carolina runs a sociology degree course dedicated to the life and work of Lady Gaga, called "Lady Gaga and the Sociology of the Fame."

⚐ SHARK ROCK Matt Waller, a shark tour operator in South Australia's Neptune Bay, has found that great white sharks are attracted by the music of Australian rock band AC/DC. Using underwater speakers attached to diving cages, he pumped rock hits through the ocean, but whereas most had little effect, when the great whites heard AC/DC they quickly swam over and rubbed their jaws against the source of the music.

⚐ PSYCHIC POWERS Don Van Vliet, the U.S. rock musician known as Captain Beefheart who died in 2010, could allegedly change TV channels using nothing more than his psychic powers, according to producer Richard Perry. Perry said that Beefheart could do this in unfamiliar environments where he had no opportunity to conceal a remote control beforehand.

DANNY FRASIER, A LEGLESS MAN FROM ALABAMA, PERFORMS AS THE WORLD'S SMALLEST ELVIS.

⚐ MONEY TO BURN In 1994, the KLF (a U.K. music duo consisting of Bill Drummond and Jimmy Cauty) burned £1 million in cash of their own money and filmed it as an art project.

⚐ TAYLOR MADE All 14 tracks from U.S. singer Taylor Swift's album *Speak Now* charted on the Billboard Top 100. For the week of November 13, 2010, she had no fewer than 11 singles on the Hot 100.

⚐ MILKING THE JOKE British comedian Milton Jones performed a stand-up routine to a field of cows on a farm in Hertfordshire, England, to see if they have a sense of humor. His set, called "Pull the Udder One," contained jokes tailored specially for his four-legged audience. Cows are believed to be more productive if they are happy.

⚐ UP HOUSE With an asking price of $400,000, U.S. firm Bangerter Homes has built an authentic replica of Carl Fredricksen's flying house from the Disney/Pixar movie *Up* at Herriman, Utah—complete with 1950s décor.

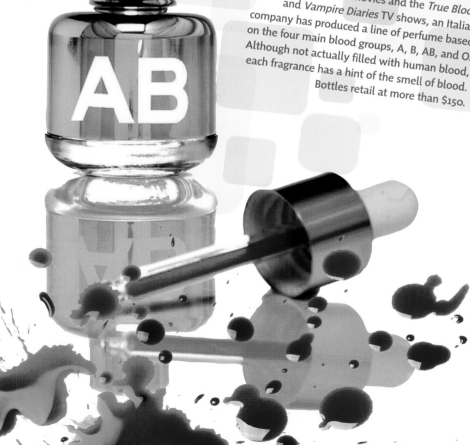

R CHUTE GOWN In 1947, Ruth Hensinger got married in a dress made from the parachute that had saved the life of her husband three years earlier. Major Claude Hensinger was returning from a bombing raid over Yowata, Japan, in August 1944 when his plane caught fire and he had to activate his parachute. Decades after Ruth walked up the aisle at Neffs, Pennsylvania, in her parachute gown, her daughter and her son's bride both wore it at their own weddings.

ROCKY RIDE

Rocky Taylor, the oldest stuntman in Britain, has finally completed the stunt (left) that was almost the end of him when he first attempted it in 1985. The 64-year-old leapt from a 40-ft-high (12-m) flaming platform into a vast pile of cardboard boxes at London's Battersea Power Station in August 2011. On set for the 1985 movie *Death Wish 3*, Taylor made the same leap from a burning building, but an explosion sent him crashing into the ground (above), inflicting multiple broken bones and burns. The Hollywood veteran made his name in the James Bond movie series and has worked on more than 100 movies, including the Indiana Jones, Pirates of the Caribbean, and Harry Potter series.

R FIVE DEATHS Hong Kong actor Law Lok Lam died in five different TV soap operas in a 24-hour period in April 2011. One character died in a fight, the second fatally vomited blood, the third succumbed to an illness, and although two more died offscreen, their deaths were discussed by other characters.

R FRIENDS TRIBUTE A working replica of the *Friends* coffee house, Central Perk, has been created in Beijing, China, because the U.S. TV comedy series is so popular there.

R POTTER MAGIC In July 2011, the opening weekend box-office takings of the movie *Harry Potter and the Deathly Hallows: Part 2* were $169 million in the United States and $307 million internationally, giving it the then new opening-weekend record in both groups.

R PRECIOUS WORDS The manuscript of an unfinished novel by 19th-century English writer Jane Austen sold for $1.6 million in London in July 2011. Every page of the manuscript—for an 1804 novel entitled *The Watsons*—is littered with crossings out, revisions, and additions, and is one of only a handful of Austen's draft works to have survived.

SCENT OF BLOOD

Perhaps inspired by the popular appetite for the *Twilight* vampire movies and the *True Blood* and *Vampire Diaries* TV shows, an Italian company has produced a line of perfume based on the four main blood groups, A, B, AB, and O. Although not actually filled with human blood, each fragrance has a hint of the smell of blood. Bottles retail at more than $150.

WAX CHAMP

World light-heavyweight boxing champion Bernard Hopkins was cast for a full-size wax figure at Ripley's Believe It or Not! world headquarters in Orlando, Florida, in August 2011. Hopkins became the oldest boxer ever to win a world title when he defeated Jean Pascal on May 21, 2011. The process of immortalizing him in wax, however, was not a quick one, taking more than two days to complete.

First, Hopkins had a thick layer of special silicone applied to his head. When this had set, cast strips were added and left to dry. Then the entire piece was removed and the process repeated for the rest of his body—taking two days. With the body casting complete, artists at Ripley's had an exact blueprint of Hopkins to use for the clay modeling and wax figure-making process. The silicone molds were precise down to his wrinkles, whiskers, and even the pores in his skin.

STRAIGHT OLLIES On July 16, 2011, Eric Carlin, 18, of Mount Laurel, Pennsylvania, strung together a record 247 straight ollies on a skateboard without his feet ever touching the ground. An ollie is a trick where the rider and skateboard leap into the air without the rider using his or her hands.

HIGH GROUND Pakistan stages a polo tournament high up on the Shandur Mountain Pass—12,251 ft (3,734 m) above sea level—in which teams from the towns on either side, Gilgit and Chitral, play each other every year.

SNOWSHOE RACE The midwinter La Ciaspolada foot race in Italy has been held annually since 1972, with its contestants wearing snowshoes from start to finish. It is run over a 5-mi (8-km) course in the Dolomite Mountains and attracts up to 6,000 entrants each year.

FISHERMAN'S FRIEND Heather, a 40-year-old, 52-lb (23.6-kg) carp living in a pond in Hampshire, England, had been caught and released hundreds of times before she was found dead in 2010.

MULTINATIONAL MATCH The English Premier League soccer match between Blackburn Rovers and West Bromwich Albion on January 23, 2011, featured players representing an amazing 22 different countries.

TRIPLE BACKFLIP On May 28, 2011, BMX rider Jed Mildon landed the world's first triple backflip at Unit T3 Mindtricks BMX Jam in his hometown of Taupo, New Zealand. He nailed the record-breaking jump by riding down a 66-ft-high (20-m) ramp carved into a hillside.

MONKEY SECURITY Indian authorities used 38 trained gray langur monkeys during the 2010 Commonwealth Games in Delhi to frighten away other monkeys from the athletes' village.

FISHERMAN'S FRIEND Heather, a 40-year-old, 52-lb (23.6-kg) carp living in a pond in Hampshire, England, had been caught and released hundreds of times before she was found dead in 2010.

GOAT GRABBING Buzkashi is a traditional Central Asian sport—and the national sport in Afghanistan—that uses a headless goat carcass as a ball. Teams on horseback try to grab the carcass from the ground and pitch it into a scoring area. Players usually wear heavy protective clothing, as the sport can be very dangerous. The winning team get to boil and eat the carcass.

PINBALL PARK

Skateboarders and BMX riders ride around a giant pinball machine at a park in Auckland, New Zealand, as if they are tiny pinballs. They are given a push down the first hill by a huge "arm" and, just like in a real pinball game, they can build up points by jumping over bleepers and bouncing off flippers.

HEAVY HULK

This sculpture of the Hulk is made entirely out of car parts! Edward Meyer, Ripley's archivist, was in Thailand looking for a transformer in 2011, when he came across the company that created the Hulk, Art from Steel. They were located in the jungle two hours from Bangkok. Ripley's have since commissioned 40 pieces from the company over the last three years, including a Godzilla, a dragon, and a snake. The Hulk is the heaviest piece, weighing more than two tons!

R TIME WARP 46-year-old Michael McTigue of West Yorkshire, England, loves the 1930s so much that all of his clothes and home furnishings are a tribute to Britain on the eve of World War II. He doesn't own a washing machine—preferring to use an old-fashioned tub and mangle—he has a vintage telephone, gramophone, and radio, and his Hoover vacuum cleaner dates from 1938.

R BOND BONANZA While clearing out the home of Marie Veloso's late mother in Saugus, Massachusetts, junk dealer Leo Guarente found an envelope containing 21 US savings bonds that cost $1,000 each when they were bought in 1972 but were worth $114,000 40 years later. He immediately presented the surprise bonds to Mrs. Veloso.

Angry Birds Live

In 2011, for one day only, Finnish company Rovio—the creators of the mobile app game phenomenon Angry Birds—collaborated with leading telecoms company Deutsche Telekom for a big ad campaign that saw them create a real-life Angry Birds game on a huge scale in Barcelona, Spain. Passersby could play the game as usual on a smartphone, but instead of watching the birds on the screen, an air-cannon propelled giant versions of the Angry Bird characters into a purpose-built fort on the street, and the birds and pigs genuinely exploded.

R ONE STEP AHEAD John and Janys Warren, from Weston-super-Mare, Somerset, England, live every winter one hour ahead of the rest of the U.K. because they think it is good for their health. Since 2006, they have lived by British Summertime all year round to combat Mr. Warren's cluster headaches, a painful condition that is thought to be triggered by a change in the clocks.

R GUILTY CONSCIENCE A barrister who stole 79 cents from a wishing fountain in Queensland, Australia, turned himself in 20 years later. Simon Matters was 19 when he took the coins in 1992 but after entering a career in the law, he finally decided to confess to the theft. The court ordered that no conviction be recorded.

R IDENTICAL BIRTHDAYS Against odds of 17 million to one, the identical twin daughters of Tracey and Davood Bageban from Gateshead, England, share a birthday with the couple's identical twin sons. The boys, Diego and Armani, were born on February 27, 2008, and daughters Dolcie and Elisia were born on the same date three years later in 2011.

R MILITARY TOMBSTONES Jason Blackburn, of Memphis, Tennessee, discovered 20 buried military tombstones, all dating back to the 1970s, while digging in his yard in May 2012.

R HUMAN SKULLS 74-year-old Anna Hoffman, a self-confessed witch from New Zealand, has a collection of more than 20 human skulls—and she claims one of them is that of notorious Australian outlaw Ned Kelly who was hanged in 1880. His skeleton was discovered in a mass grave in Melbourne in 2009, but much of his skull was missing.

R SKIN SHOES Following the 1881 public hanging of outlaw George "Big Nose" Parrot in Carbon County, Wyoming, a local doctor had his skin made into a pair of dress shoes and a medical bag. The top of Parrott's skull was also sawn off and the cap was presented to a 15-year-old female medical assistant who used it variously as an ashtray, a pen holder, and a doorstop.

R FAMILY REUNION Minoru Ohye, of West Sacramento, California, celebrated his 86th birthday by traveling to Kyoto, Japan, to be reunited with his brother, Hiroshi Kamimura, after nearly 60 years of separation. The brothers were born in Sacramento but were separated as children after their father died in a fishing accident. They were then sent to live with relatives in Japan but ended up in different homes. Phone conversations between the two were awkward as, unusually for brothers, they spoke different languages, Kamimura being unable to understand English.

R PERSISTANT CALLER In September 2011, police in Rotterdam, the Netherlands, charged a woman with stalking after she had called a man 65,000 times in a year—an average of 178 times a day, or about once every eight minutes.

THE STATS

- Around one person in 14, globally, has downloaded Angry Birds, equivalent to seven percent of the world's population.
- Worldwide, people spend 300 million minutes every day playing Angry Birds—or 24 years of game play in every hour.
- Angry Birds has had more than two billion sales (counting downloads as sales); that's more than Call of Duty, Halo, Sonic the Hedgehog, Grand Theft Auto, and Mario Kart combined.
- Angry Birds has been the number one paid app game in 79 countries.
- In total, at least 400 billion angry birds have been launched at the green pigs' castles, and almost 300 billion levels completed.
- Angry Birds cost €100,000 and six months to build. It was the 52nd game developed by Finnish company Rovio.

APPY BIRTHDAY

Mike Cooper from Kent, England, made a spectacular Angry Birds birthday cake for his son Ben when he turned six years old in 2011. Not only was it made from chocolate and sponge, it was a fully functioning Angry Birds game in itself, complete with catapult and sugary birds for catapulting. This swiftly led to a demolition and devouring of the cake, which had taken Mike ten hours to make.

DARING STUNT

A daredevil driver in Florida calmly maneuvered his Mazda car under a moving 18-wheel juggernaut traveling at a speed of around 40 mph (65 km/h)... and stayed there for over a minute. His reckless action, captured on film by a shocked motorist, mimics a scene from the 2001 movie *The Fast and the Furious*, where actor Vin Diesel drives underneath a truck that his gang is trying to rob.

PERFECT PARKING German stunt driver Ronny Wechselberger squeezed his Volkswagen Polo car into a parking space that was just 10¼ in (26 cm) longer than his vehicle. He performed the incredible feat of parallel parking by using the handbrake to flick the car's rear end around.

MINI CHOPPER U.S. company Vanguard Defense Industries has developed a remote-controlled helicopter that is being used to track pirates off East Africa and tackle crime in the United States. The Shadowhawk UAV is just 7 ft (2.1 m) long and weighs 49 lb (22 kg), but it has a top speed of 70 mph (112 km/h). It can fire tasers, grenades, and shotgun shells, and record and broadcast footage in real time.

JEEP RECORD On August 12, 2011, more than 1,100 Jeeps from across the United States converged on the Bantam Heritage Jeep Festival at Butler, Pennsylvania, to break the record for the world's largest Jeep parade.

TRAFFIC DIRECTOR Civilian Hugh McManaway spent so much of his spare time directing traffic at a busy intersection that the city of Charlotte, North Carolina, built a statue to commemorate him.

NEW ROADS Although it already has 2 million mi (3.2 million km) of road, placing it third in the world behind the United States and China, India is building another 15 mi (24 km) of road every day to cater for the nation's rapidly expanding use of cars.

FIRST BAN Venezuela issued its first-ever driving ban in 2011—to a bus driver who was speeding in an overladen, six-wheel passenger bus that was missing one of its rear wheels. Drivers have strong rights in Venezuela, where the first law allowing the ban of motorists was not introduced until 2008, and the bus driver's ban was suspended for 12 months.

BABY DRIVER A seven-year-old Michigan boy, who had to stand up to reach the gas and brake pedals, drove over 20 mi (32 km) in an attempt to see his father. The boy took his stepfather's Pontiac Sunfire and, barefoot and in pajamas, hit speeds of 70 mph (113 km/h) before being stopped by a police patrol.

THINK BIKE Toyota has created a bicycle with gears you can change by using your mind. The rider of the Prius X Parlee (PXP) wears a special "neuron helmet" that uses electrodes to pick up cues from the brain and send signals to a thought-controlled gearbox mounted under the seat of the bicycle.

FIRE DRILL A team of 25 firefighters from London, England, drove 30,000 mi (48,000 km) around the world—in a fire engine named *Martha*. Their nine-month journey took them through 28 countries, including Russia, China, Australia, New Zealand, and the United States.

LOW CAR Students from Okayama Sanyo High School in Asakuchi, Japan, built a single-seater electric car that is just 18 in (45 cm) high and runs at speeds of up to 30 mph (50 km/h).

Ferrari Table

French furniture designer Charly Molinelli has encased the wreck of a Ferrari F40 supercar in a coffee table. Asked to build a unique piece and knowing that his client was a motor-sports fan, Molinelli approached a friend who worked at a scrapyard that was crushing a Ferrari and managed to procure it.

VERTICAL PARKING

Heralding today's multistory parking lots, in the early 1920s cars were hoisted up on individual platforms to form elevator-style parking lots in order to save space.

Sweet Suckers

This slippery customer is actually a cleverly constructed cake. Karen Portaleo of the Highland Bakery in Atlanta, Georgia, is a former clay sculptor who has applied her creative talents to incredible cake decorations. The body and tentacles of the octopus were built with layers of sponge cake before being shaped, covered with fondant, and airbrushed. The sponge giant weighed 200 lb (90 kg) and was devoured within two days of being created.

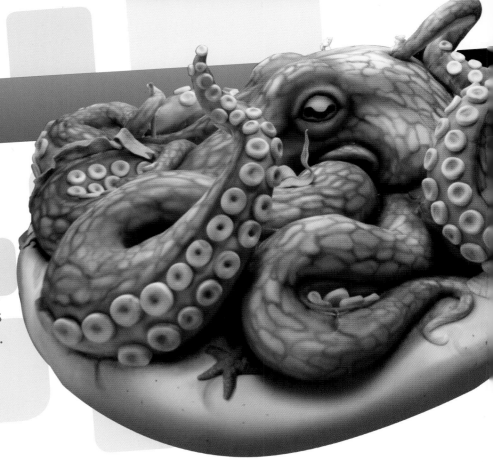

☒ CICADA DESSERT In 2011, an ice-cream shop in Columbia, Missouri, prepared cicada ice cream—and sold out of it within hours. Employees at Sparky's Homemade Ice Cream collected the cicadas in their backyards and removed the wings. They then boiled the bugs and coated them in brown sugar and milk chocolate before adding them to the brown sugar and butter ice-cream base.

☒ COSTLY KEBAB Chef Andy Bates from London, England, served up a £750 ($1,100) kebab, made from expensive purple violet potatoes, *coeur de boeuf* tomatoes, milk-fed lamb, and a mint yogurt topping infused with luxurious Krug champagne.

☒ CHOCOLATE TREE French chocolatier Patrick Roger created a chocolate Christmas tree, 33-ft-high (10-m) and weighing more than four tons, in his Paris laboratory.

☒ BUMPER B.L.T. In Kansas City in 2011, volunteers assembled a bacon, lettuce, and tomato sandwich that was 209 ft (63.7 m) long. It took 14 people 42 minutes to prepare the sandwich, using 3,300 slices of bacon, seven cases of lettuce, and 750 lb (340 kg) of tomatoes.

☒ BIRTHDAY CAKE To celebrate Canada's 144th birthday on July 1, 2011, three bakeries in Toronto, Ontario, joined forces to create a cake over 5 ft (1.5 m) tall, with 255 layers. The giant confection required 287 lb (130 kg) of sugar and copious amounts of eggs, flour, and butter.

☒ OLD CAKE In 2010, Justin Agrella of San Leandro, California, discovered a steamer trunk belonging to his grandparents with a well-preserved piece of their 96-year-old wedding cake inside.

☒ LIZARD LUNCH A lizard commonly eaten in restaurants across southeast Vietnam is an all-female species unknown to science until 2010. *Leiolepis ngovantrii*, which reproduces itself by cloning, was finally discovered on a lunch buffet menu by scientists.

☒ MOUSE MENACE Shopping at a supermarket in Birmingham, England, Liz Wray was horrified to see half a dozen live baby mice fall out of a packet of potato chips she had just picked up.

☒ SQUID BOTTLE An Ika Tokkuri is a Japanese liquor bottle that has been made from an entire sun-dried squid. The cleaned and dried squid skin is often stuffed with rice or grain to help it form a bottle shape, and when sake is poured into it, the drink absorbs the flavor of the squid. The bottle can be reused up to six times, after which it can be eaten!

CHEESY OUTFITS

Students from Bath Spa University, England, spent 1,000 hours making five dresses from a ton of cheese. Their designs included shoes made of cheese and dresses encrusted with heat-molded, sculpted Cheddar.

WEIRD CAKES
Other crazy cake creations from around the world include...

- **BABY GIRAFFE**
Debbie Goard of Oakland, California, made a baby giraffe cake 2-ft-tall (60-cm).

- **ST. PAUL'S CATHEDRAL**
George D'Aubney built a 4-ft-tall (1.2-m) fruitcake replica of the famous cathedral in London, England.

- **STATE OF TEXAS**
Gladys Farek from Cistern, Texas, made a fruitcake measuring 5 x 6 ft (1.5 x 1.8 m) in the shape of her home state.

- **BRIDE IN DRESS**
When Chidi and Innocent Ogbuta of Dallas, Texas, renewed their wedding vows, they ordered a 400-lb (180-kg) butterscotch cake that was a life-size model of Chidi in her bridal dress.

- **FULL-SIZE SKODA CAR**
Made by a team of British bakers for a successful ad campaign.

- **LIFE-SIZE HUMAN CHEST ORGANS**
Created by horror fan Barbara Jo of San Jose, California.

SALAD DRESSING To encourage Chinese people to adopt a meat-free diet—meat consumption in the country has quadrupled over the course of the last 40 years—actress Gao Yuanyuan wore a gown made of lettuce and cabbage leaves topped with a necklace fashioned from red chili peppers. Gao herself had stopped eating meat after her pet dog suffered food poisoning two years earlier.

HEAVY CAKE A total of 100 workers from Dairy Queen, Canada, spent 14 hours in a Toronto, Ontario, square in May 2011 assembling an ice-cream cake that weighed more than 10 tons. The cake contained over 20,000 lb (9,070 kg) of ice cream, 200 lb (91 kg) of sponge cake, and 300 lb (136 kg) of icing and crumble. The gigantic dessert was created to celebrate the 30th birthday of Dairy Queen's much-loved ice-cream cake.

SOAP EATER A rare and dangerous medical condition left Tempestt Henderson, a teenage girl from Florida, addicted to eating soap. She used to go through five bars of soap a week, as well as devouring washing powder daily, and licking soap bubbles off her skin in the shower. Doctors diagnosed her as suffering from pica, a condition that causes people to eat substances with no nutritional value, such as chalk, metal, and sand.

MEALWORM MORSELS

Mealworm quiches and grasshopper spring rolls are among the edible delights created by Dutch scientist Arnold van Huis who has teamed up with a cooking school in Wageningen, the Netherlands, to produce a cookbook of tasty insect recipes. Van Huis believes that bug-eating is the future of nutrition, and that increased bug consumption will help alleviate global food shortages, as well as reduce carbon emissions created by other foodstuffs.

Zombie Prank

Don't be alarmed! The warning of zombies ahead that greeted drivers in southern Ontario, Canada, in May 2011 was not caused by an invasion of the walking dead but by pranksters hacking into electronic road signs. Similar warnings have appeared on electronic signs in a number of U.S. states, including Illinois where, in 2009, rush-hour motorists near Collinsville were urged to exercise caution because of "DAILY LANE CLOSURES DUE TO ZOMBIES."

PERFECT GAMES Eighty-five-year-old John Bates of Onalaska, Wisconsin, has bowled more than 3,200 perfect games—ones that consist entirely of strikes—in Wii Sports bowling. He plays about 20 games of Wii bowling a day.

PRESIDENTIAL PRANK "Rickrolling" is an Internet phenomenon in which an unsuspecting user who clicks on a link is directed to the video of Rick Astley's 1987 hit "Never Gonna Give You Up." When David Wiggs from Tennessee complained in July 2011 that the White House Twitter feed on U.S. debt was dull, the White House "rickrolled" him by suggesting he click on the link that led to Astley's video.

RINGING CROC A cell phone kept ringing inside the stomach of a crocodile after a woman accidentally dropped it into the enclosure while trying to take a photo. Gena, a 14-year-old croc at the Dnipropetrovsk Oceanarium, Ukraine, refused food and began acting listlessly after swallowing the phone. The woman said she wanted her SIM card back as it contained her contacts.

BEER CANNON Technology consultant Ryan Rusnak from Tyson's Corner, Virginia, has designed the Beer Bot, an iPhone-controlled refrigerator that uses a compressed air cannon to fire cans of cold beer across a room into waiting arms. The fridge is fitted with an ioBridge microcontroller, a device that allows the fridge to link to Ryan's iPhone via the Internet.

ROYAL KISS The royal wedding of Prince William and Kate Middleton on April 29, 2011, in the U.K. had 72 million views on YouTube by people in 188 countries. During the newlyweds' ten-second balcony kiss, the YouTube channel experienced an additional 100,000 requests on top of the already high load—that's an extra 10,000 requests per second.

SCARY NOSE A 2011 YouTube clip of Emerson, a five-and-a-half-month-old baby boy from London, Canada, freaking out at the sound of his mother blowing her nose went viral, racking up over two million views in its first three days online. After just four months, more than 21 million people had watched it.

FACEBOOK FUGITIVE A man wanted in Utica, New York State, used his Facebook page to taunt police, "Catch me if you can, I'm in Brooklyn." NYPD detectives said they tracked Victor Burgos down to a Brooklyn apartment where they found him sitting at his computer with his Facebook page open.

BOUGHT TOWN Maddie and Neal Love bought the entire town of Wauconda, Washington State, on eBay for $360,000. The remote outpost has a gas pump, a restaurant, a small store, a four-bedroom house, and its own ZIP code. At its peak in the early 20th century, the former mining town had several hundred residents.

HARDY IMITATION A Canadian Laurel and Hardy fan has been posted on Twitter because of her distinctive name—Laurel-Ann Hardie. A professor at Fanshawe College in London, Ontario, the former Laurel-Ann Hasen realized she would be subjected to attention when she married James Hardie.

SUPER MARIO Born in 1985, the same year that Nintendo introduced the first Super Mario Bros. game, Mitsugu Kikai from Tokyo, Japan, has since collected more than 5,400 items of Super Mario memorabilia.

TOILET GAMES

Male toilet users in Tokyo, Japan, can play urine-controlled video games. The SEGA game, Toylets, operates via a pressure sensor mounted on the back of the urinal that measures the strength and accuracy of the user's urine jet. A small L.C.D. screen at eye level then allows him to play various games, including using his urine to erase virtual graffiti from a wall, and measuring how much pee has accurately hit the sensor.

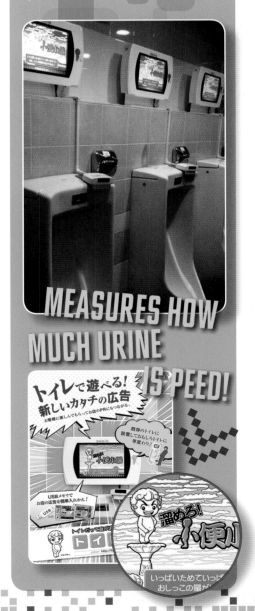

MEASURES HOW MUCH URINE IS PEED!

Claiming to be the inventor of planking, Andy Welch, who now lives in Sussex, England, planks face up as well as face down.

EXTREME PLANKING

Planking is a worldwide craze that has taken off dramatically in recent years due to plankers posting their images on the Internet. The phenomenon involves participants lying face down in unusual locations with their hands touching the sides of the body—mimicking a wooden plank—while someone else takes a picture of the event.

Several people claim to have invented planking, including New Zealander Andy Welch, who says he invented the original craze while on vacation in Croatia in 2006 after he and his girlfriend became bored with striking the usual poses for holiday photos.

Famous plankers include Orlando Magic basketball star Dwight Howard, who planked with 100 fans on a basketball court in Beijing, China, in September 2011 to form the initials "D.H.," and Max Key, son of New Zealand's prime minister John Key, who planked along the back of a sofa with his father standing behind him in May 2011.

Extreme planker Simon Carville from Perth, Australia, once posted a Facebook photo of himself lying naked and rigidly horizontal while being held aloft in the arms of Eliza, a 7.2-ft-high (2.2-m) iconic city statue.

Vincent Migliore demonstrates his planking skills on a tree stump in a city park in Folsom, California, in August 2011.

Reuben Wilson planks on Cairns Esplanade, Queensland, Australia, in May 2011.

Taiwan's most famous plankers are the Pujie Girls (meaning "Falling on the Street" in Mandarin). They say they wish to use the craze and their associated fame to spread positive social messages.

美味しい
* Вкусно по-японски

A Russian planker photographed by Tima Sergeev is seen here planking on an advertising sign in St. Petersburg, Russia.

Чикен Шейк
Вкусно

FRISBEE CATCH A video clip of probably the greatest frisbee catch ever notched up 1.5-million hits in just three days on YouTube. Standing on a bridge 50 ft (15 m) above the Swan River in Perth, Western Australia, Brodie Smith hurled the frisbee 500 ft (150 m) out across the water, where Derek Herron leaped 6 ft (1.8 m) from a moving speedboat to make a spectacular one-handed, midair catch.

SOCCER TWEETS Japan's penalty shoot-out victory over the U.S. in the FIFA Women's World Cup soccer final in Frankfurt, Germany, on July 17, 2011, prompted Twitter users to tweet in overdrive. At their peak, tweeters were sending 7,196 tweets per second.

PETS' PAGES One in ten of all U.K. pets have their own Facebook page, Twitter profile, or YouTube channel, and more than half of pet owners in the U.K. post about their animals on Internet social networks.

HOLLYWOOD DEAL Just four days after uploading a short film to YouTube in November 2009, Uruguayan director Fede Alvarez was being courted by every studio in Hollywood—and within a month he had been offered a $30-million contract to make a Hollywood sci-fi movie. His film, *Ataque de Pánico!* (*Panic Attack!*), featured giant robots destroying Uruguay's capital city, Montevideo. Running for less than five minutes, it was made on a budget of just $300. It has had more than 6.8 million views on YouTube.

APP TO RESCUE After a Polish trucker was involved in a road crash near Colchester, England, in July 2011, quick-thinking paramedic Nicola Draper downloaded an iPhone app so that she could treat him. When she realized the driver did not speak English, she searched for the online medical Polish translator tool.

VIRTUAL CITY Kevin Alderman of Tampa, Florida, built a digital simulation of the city of Amsterdam in the online game Second Life and subsequently sold the virtual property on eBay for $50,000.

YELLER PAGES Johnathan "Fatal1ty" Wendel from Independence, Missouri, has won over $500,000 by competing in professional gaming competitions. He set a world record for the game Quake, with a massive 671 kills in 60 minutes.

YOUR UPLOADS

www.ripleys.com/submit

Joe Pires of Geneva, Florida, has a home with a stunning trick up its sleeve; it doubles as a hangar large enough to fit an airplane. The façade of the building hinges electronically to reveal a large hangar for various flying craft. Joe can jump into a gyrocopter or microlight without leaving his home, and taxi straight out onto the runway, which also doubles as his lawn.

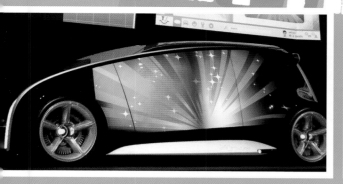

JUSTIN'S KLOUT The San Francisco-based social networking index Klout has calculated that Canadian teenage pop star Justin Bieber is more influential online than the Dalai Lama or Barack Obama. Klout adds up tweets, likes, pings, LinkedIn connections, Google mentions, status updates, and other social media data to measure a person's importance online.

FAST FINGERS In July 2011, 15-year-old Eduard Saakashvili, son of the President of Georgia, typed the entire English alphabet (A to Z) on an iPad's software keyboard in just 5.26 seconds.

TOTALLY BATTY When a group of students called the "Batman Boilers," from Purdue University, Indiana, posted a YouTube video of themselves hanging upside down by their feet—like bats—from the tops of walls, gates, fences, statues, and street signs, it led to a new Internet craze. "Batmanning" was inspired partly by "planking," in which people are photographed face down in unusual places.

ORIGINAL NAME Lior and Vardit Adler of Hod Hasharon, Israel, named their daughter after a feature on the social networking site Facebook. They called her Like in honour of a button on the site that allows users to express their approval of photographs, links, comments, and status updates.

PS2 COLLECTOR A dedicated gamer for more than 19 years, games fanatic "Ahans76" has collected every PlayStation 2 game ever released in North America—a total of over 1,850. He has spent around $60,000 on his collection, but got lucky when, having searched for years for an early, sealed "Moto GP" game, a U.K. user sold it to him for $9 on eBay.

PLAYING WITH FIRE An enterprising trombone player called Scott, from Jackson, Missouri, has fitted up his trombone with a gas tank so that it also serves as a flamethrower. His YouTube video shows him shooting out 21-ft-long (6.4-m) jets of fire while playing his "Flamebone."

MAGIC MOTOR

Toyota has created a car that can change its entire appearance at the touch of a button. The body of the hi-tech Fun-Vii is made of touch-screen panels that allow the driver to alter the pattern on display in an instant, like a smartphone. The car even flashes up a greeting message to the driver on the door.

CELEBRITY CAT The escapades of Maru the cat have been viewed more than 141 million times on YouTube. Described by his Japanese owner as "a little bumbling and a little awkward," Maru has been filmed in more than 200 videos, and has attracted around 190,000 subscribers who have signed up to be notified of his next adventure.

Index

goat carcass, used as ball 22
Gobitaca, Alassan Issa (Swe) 14, 14
gorilla, dancing 14, 14

H
Hardie, Laurel-Ann (Can) 30
head
   dislocated from spine 10
   turning 180 degrees 15
helicopters, miniature 26
Hensinger, Major Claude (USA) 21
Hensinger, Ruth (USA) 21
Herron, Derek (Aus) 32
Heuschkel, Melissa (Ger) 18
Hitler, Adolf (Aut) 18
Hoffman, Anna (NZ) 25
Holmes, Michael (NZ) 15
Hopkins, Bernard (USA) 22, 22
horsemaning 9, 9
Hosie, Wesley (UK) 16
hot dogs, stuffing into T-shirt 16
houses
   airplane built in basement 12
   as airplane hangar 32, 32–33
   replica of flying house 20
Howard, Dwight (USA) 31
Huis, Arnold van (Nld) 29, 29
Hulk, made of car parts 24, 24

I
ice cream 28, 29
insects, eating 29, 29
Internet
   "Batmanning" 33
   influential people on 33
   pets on social networks 32
   "Rickrolling" 30
   wacky websites 18
iPad, fast typing on 33
iPhones
   app helps crash victim 32
   blows air 8
   boy designs video games 8
   food covers 8, 8
   strange apps 19
   see also cell phones

J
Janus, Tim "Eater X" (USA) 16
Jeeps, mass parade of 26
jelly bean, image of Kate Middleton on 16
jewelry, octopus necklace 16, 16
Jo, Barbara (USA) 29
Joiner, Ginny (USA) 14
Jones, Milton (UK) 20

K
Kamimura, Hiroshi (Jap) 25
kebab, very expensive 28
Key, Max (NZ) 31
Kikai, Mitsugu (Jap) 30
kissing, royal wedding 30
Kumar, Harsh (Ind) 10

L
Lady Gaga (USA) 20, 20
Langston, Jacob (USA) 15
Laurel and Hardy 30
Law Lok Lam (Chn) 21
legless Elvis impersonator 20
life, selling on eBay 18
lizards, rare lizard found on restaurant menu 28
Love, Maddie and Neal (USA) 30
Luo Yanbo (Chn) 10

M
McCurdy, Elmer (USA) 10
McDonald's 17
McIntosh, Richard (USA) 6
McManaway, Hugh (USA) 26
McTigue, Michael (UK) 24
Mahler, Robert (USA) 9
manhole, exploding 13
manure, sold on eBay 19
maps, Google maps blamed for military invasion 8
market, train runs through 12, 12–13
marriage proposals
   on bus display sign 13
   on movie screen 14
Mary, Virgin, cheese sandwich with likeness of 18
Matters, Simon (Aus) 25
mealworms, eating 29, 29
meat, dress made of 20, 20
mice, in potato chip packet 28
Mickey Mouse, potato in shape of 19
Middleton, Kate (UK) 16, 30
Migliore, Vincent (USA) 31, 31
Mildon, Jed (NZ) 22
Molinelli, Charly (Fra) 26, 26
money, burning as art project 20
monkeys, as guards 22
Morgan, Adrian (USA) 16
motorcycle, rider impaled 10
mountain, high-level polo tournament 22
movies
   dummies as extras 6–7, 6–7
   huge box-office takings 21

movies (cont.)
   marriage proposal on movie screen 14
   replica of flying house 20
music
   popular album 20
   sharks like rock music 20
   trombone as flamethrower 33

N
names
   Laurel and Hardy fan 30
   rights sold on eBay 18
necklace, octopus 16, 16
Nicora, Nick (USA) 17
nose
   blowing freaks baby 30
   objects hammered into 10
novel, valuable manuscript 21

O
octopuses
   as necklace 16, 16
   octopus-shaped cake 28, 28
Ogbuta, Chidi and Innocent (USA) 29
Ohye, Minoru (USA) 25
old-fashioned lifestyle 24
Openshaw, Phill (UK) 13
orangutan, rescues chick 14

P
Pacino, Al (USA) 19, 19
painkiller, pineapple as 16
Pakravan, Reza (UK) 13
Pandey, Shruti (Ind) 10
parachute, dress made from 21
Parrot, George (USA) 25
Pascal, Jean (Hai) 22
perfume, blood-scented 21, 21
Perry, Richard (USA) 20
pinball machine, skateboarders on giant 23, 23
pineapple, as painkiller 16
pipe, swimmer sucked into 10
pirates, miniature helicopter tracks 26
Pires, Joe (USA) 32, 32–33
planking 31, 31, 33
police 18, 30
polo, high-level tournament 22
Portaleo, Karen 28, 28
potato, in shape of Mickey Mouse 19
Presley, Elvis (USA) 19, 20
prisons 16, 18
Pujie Girls (Twn) 31, 31

Q
Qiu Sheng (Chn) 10

R
raft, crossing Atlantic on 12
Reeves, Dan (USA) 12
refrigerator, fires beer cans 30
restaurants
   customers eat in cars 17
   popularity of McDonald's 17
   rare lizard found on menu 28
   turns royalty away 16
   twins restaurant 16
   wall of books 16
rice, giant sushi rolls 16
Riddle, Paul (USA) 9
road signs, zombie warnings 30, 30
road sweeper, tai chi routine 15
roads, building in India 26
rock music, sharks like 20
Roger, Patrick (Fra) 28
Ross, Gary (USA) 6
Rusnak, Ryan (USA) 30

S
Saakashvili, Eduard (Geo) 33
sandwiches
   enormous 16, 28
   sold on eBay 18
Schellenberger, Nadine (Ger) 16
screwdrivers, tricycle powered by 13
seaweed dress 16, 16
Sergeev, Tima (Rus) 31, 31
sharks
   dog bites 14
   jumps over surfer 15
   like rock music 20
shoe, giant shoe as car 13
Silvia, Queen of Sweden 16
Silviak, Paul (USA) 9
skateboards 22, 23, 23
skin, made into shoes and bag 25
skulls, collection of human 25
skydiving, lucky escape 15
Smith, Anthony (UK) 12
Smith, Brodie (Aus) 32
snowballs, sold on eBay 19
snowman, bus driver runs over 14
snowshoe race 22
soap, eating 29
soap operas, multiple deaths for character 21
soccer 18, 22, 32
socks, dirty socks sold on eBay 19
spam sandwich, enormous 16
Spears, Britney (USA) 19

ACKNOWLEDGMENTS

Front cover (b) Jill Johnson; **4** Albert Tan; **6–7** Courtesy of the Inflatable Crowd Company; **8** Strapya/Rex Features; **9** (c) Jeffrey Bautista , (t) Brent Douglas, (b) Deney Tuazon; **11** (r) Dragstrip/Solent News/Rex Features, (t/l, b/l) Solent News/Rex Features; **12** (t) Albert Tan , (b) www.julienberthier.org courtesy galerie GP&N Vallois, Paris ; **13** (l, c, r) http://www.stanley.sg, (b) © Photoshot/TIPS; **14** (t) Courtesy of Alassan Issa Gobitaca , (b) Courtesy of Calgary Zoo; **15** (t) Mark & Ellen Zessin/www.JennyThePug.com, (b) David Devore; **16** © Picture Alliance/Photoshot; **17** (l) Gareth Fuller/PA Wire, (c) W.C.P.C. Championship, (t/r, c/r) Gareth Fuller/PA Wire, (b/r) Chris Radburn/PA Wire; **18** (t) Jill Johnson, (b) Reuters/Danny Moloshok; **19** (b) SP/Rex Features; **20** (l) Startraks Photo/Rex Features, (sp) © Hemeroskopion/Fotolia.com; **21** (t/l, t/r) Wenn.com, (b) Rex Features, (b/r) © Anyka/Fotolia.com; **23** Caters News; **24** (b/l) Saatchi, (b/r) Courtesy of Rovio; **25** (c/l, b/l) Courtesy of Rovio, (c/r) Mike Cooper/Electricpig.co.uk; **26** (t) Swns.com, (b) Charly Molinelli/Rex Features; **27** FPG/Hulton Archive/Getty Images; **28** (t) Caters News, (b) Swns.com; **29** Reuters/Jerry Lampen; **30** (l) Phyllis Keating, (r) © 2012 Sega Corporation; **31** (t) Rex Features, (t/l) Vincent T. Migliore, (c/l) Newspix/Rex Features, (b/l) Reuters/Nicky Loh, (b) Tima Sergeev; **32–33** (t) Reuters/Kim Kyung-Hoon, (b) Courtesy of Joe Pires; **Back cover** Phyllis Keating

Key: t = top, b = bottom, c = center, l = left, r = right, sp = single page, dp = double page

All other photos are from Ripley Entertainment Inc.
Every attempt has been made to acknowledge correctly and contact copyright holders and we apologize in advance for any unintentional errors or omissions, which will be corrected in future editions.

Contents

The Color System

PAUL MITCHELL schools

PREFACE

Who Is The Color System For?

The Color System is for the brand-new learner or Future Professional eager to master the *what, why,* and *how* of hair color. Mastering these core fundamentals will give you the knowledge — not only in your head but also in your hands — to understand color formulation, placement, effect, and much more.

- How do you know whether to place color vertically, diagonally, or horizontally?
- What effect does a weave or slice create?
- What kind of color placement works best on hair that is layered, one length, or graduated?
- How do hair texture and formation affect sectioning and placement choice?
- What do you need to understand about the laws of color or light, tone, and depth?

These and many more questions will be answered in **The Color System**.

But, what if you're an experienced learner or salon professional? Will you learn from **The Color System**? Absolutely! The best action step that any seasoned hairdresser can take is to continue to return to and revisit the core fundamentals. Repetition is truly the mother of all skill!

At Paul Mitchell, general common knowledge is the goal between our Future Professionals and any experienced hairdresser currently working in a salon or backstage at a hair show or presenting a class in a hair salon or school.

The Color System will lead you in mastering the fundamentals of hair color. Come and celebrate the business and creativity of color with us. At John Paul Mitchell Systems® and Paul Mitchell Schools, we are determined to help you succeed in this wonderful industry and we are truly dedicated to providing the education that will increase your knowledge, skills, and earning potential.

The Color System

PAUL MITCHELL
schools

Introduction
Colorful Learning

Personal Learning Preferences

Thinking Process

Receiving Process

Processing and Accessing

Using and Applying Information

Stringer or Grouper? Quiz

Learning Strategy

How to Use The Color System

Colorful Learning

At Paul Mitchell Schools, we believe that every person deserves his or her own customized education. Our learning culture involves each learner by creating classes and curriculum that are full of discovery and fun.

Personal Learning Preferences

Improve your learning experience through personal learning preferences. At Paul Mitchell Schools, we help our learners discover how they learn best and encourage them to create and discover their own personal learning strategy (preferences). These learning preferences include processing, accessing, thinking, receiving, applying, and using information.

Intelligence is not about "how smart you are," it's about *how you are smart.* To be a successful learner, it's important for you to discover how you prefer to learn.

- Are you the kind of learner who likes to learn in a linear fashion with step-by-step instructions?
- Do you prefer to jump from one key point to another?
- Do you learn by watching or looking at pictures?
- Do you learn by doing, listening, or reading?
- Do you like to talk about what you are learning?
- Do you need quiet time to reflect on your learning?

There are many different ways to learn and one way is just as good as another.

Thinking Process

Understanding your thinking process will assist you in developing your learning strategy. Do you like to learn each detail or do you prefer to see the "big picture"?

A **stringer learner** prefers to focus on the details one concept at a time until he or she learns all of the information.

A **grouper learner** prefers to see all of the information in a broader spectrum and then work from the top down to the details.

To discover your preference, take the stringer/grouper quiz in this chapter.

Receiving Process

How you prefer to receive information is another important tool in developing your learning strategy. What kind of information do you prefer to receive?

- **Visual** — This includes posters, lots of color, visuals, or viewing demonstrations and DVDs.
- **Auditory** — This includes music, listening, speaking, and talking.
- **Kinesthetic** — This includes hands-on activities, touching, and doing.

Knowing your visual, auditory, or kinesthetic (VAK) preference will assist you in creating a sensory learning experience.

Processing and Accessing

Multiple Intelligence helps you to understand how you prefer to process and access information. Understanding your multiple intelligence(s) will assist you in creating and customizing a learning routine designed especially for you that will improve your learning and retention.

Dr. Howard Gardner identified at least seven different intelligences:

- **Verbal/Linguistic** — These learners understand and use communication through written and spoken word. They enjoy debate and discussion and they respond well to words both spoken and written.

- **Math/Logic** — These learners understand and communicate through numerical and graphic pathways. They want everything to add up for them and they approach an experience in a logical way.

- **Musical** — These learners understand and communicate through the language of musical notation, rhythmic patterns, and environmental sounds. They like to create their own pattern and they respond well to a specific order and rhythm to their communication and action steps.

- **Body/Kinesthetic** — These learners understand and communicate through movement and analyzing movement. They are hands-on people who possess something known as *body memory:* the more they repeat a behavior, the better they can master it.

- **Spatial** — These learners understand and use communication with charts, pictures, and the use of space. They can easily visualize solutions and they respond well to the use of art, pictures, graphs, maps, demonstrations, and mental pictures.

- **Interpersonal** — These learners understand and communicate by collaborating in groups. They are able to recognize differences in individuals, their moods, and their intentions.

- **Intrapersonal** — These learners understand and communicate with the ability to place themselves in a model or situation. They respond well to their own intuition and they need quiet time to let the information soak in.

To learn more about multiple intelligences, go to **http://www.micubed.com/1/**.

Using and Applying Information

Learning types assist you in understanding how you prefer to apply and use information.

- Do you often ask "why" when learning? Do you prefer to make a connection with information? Are you most comfortable learning in groups? You may be a *feeler* learner.

- Do you ask "what" when learning? Do you take your time to think about the information you learn? Do you make a logical or intellectual connection? Do you like to know all of the facts and details on a subject? You may be a *thinker* learner.

- Do you ask "how" when learning? Do you learn best by doing? Do you learn through practice and physical perspective? Do you like to jump right in and get your hands involved? You may be a *driver* learner.

- Do you ask "what if" when learning? Do you focus on how to improve the information by doing it differently or improve the process? Do you like to explore all possibilities? You may be an *inventor* learner.

Stringer or Grouper? Quiz

Check the phrase in each pair of questions that corresponds more closely to your preferred approach to learning. There is no right or wrong answer. The questions are designed to uncover your preferences.

1. When studying one unfamiliar subject, you…
   _____ a. Prefer to gather information from diverse topic areas.
   _____ b. Prefer to focus on one topic.

2. You would rather…
   _____ a. Know a little about a lot of different subjects.
   _____ b. Become an expert on just one subject.

3. When studying from a textbook, you…
   _____ a. Skip ahead and read chapters of special interest out of sequence.
   _____ b. Work systematically from one chapter to the next, not moving on until you understand the material.

4. When asking people for information about a subject of interest, you…
   _____ a. Tend to ask broad questions that require general answers.
   _____ b. Tend to ask narrow or specific questions that demand a detailed answer.

5. When browsing at the library, bookstore, or online, you…
   _____ a. Roam around looking at books or topics on many different subjects.
   _____ b. Stay more or less in one place, looking at books on only a few subjects.

6. You are best at remembering…
   _____ a. General principles and ideas.
   _____ b. Specific facts.

7. When performing a task, you…
   _____ a. Like to have background information not strictly related to the work.
   _____ b. Prefer to concentrate on strictly relevant information.

8. You think that educators should…
   _____ a. Give learners exposure to a wide range of subjects in school.
   _____ b. Ensure that learners mainly acquire in-depth knowledge and skill on related subjects.

Stringer or Grouper? Quiz

continued

9. When on vacation, you would rather…

    _____ a. Spend a short time in several places.

    _____ b. Stay in one place the whole time and get to know it well.

10. When learning something, you would rather…

    _____ a. Follow general guidelines.

    _____ b. Work with detailed plans of action.

11. In addition to specialized knowledge, you think people should…

    _____ a. Know some math, art, physics, literature, psychology, politics, language, biology, or history (or learn four or more subjects).

    _____ b. Focus on the concepts, skills, and knowledge that will create success for them.

- Now total all the "a" and "b" answers.
- If you scored six or more a's on this test, you are a grouper learner.
- If you scored six or more b's, you are a stringer learner.
- The higher your score, the more specialized your learning style.

Note: Test taken from *Peak Learning* by Ronald Gross.

Grouper	Stringer
Learns from the TOP DOWN	Learns from the BOTTOM UP

Learning Cycle and Types Map

Feeler

- Likes to work and learn in groups
- Learns through relationships
- Seeks an emotional connection
- Is socially aware
- Asks Why?
- Needs to find personal meaning
- Needs harmony and cooperation
- Seeks what's in it for him/her

Feelers ask "Why?" They need to know the meaning of what they are learning and how it relates to them.

Thinker

- Learns by thinking and analyzing
- Wants details
- May seek perfection
- Is intellectual
- Learns using logic
- Shows low level of emotion
- Asks What?

Thinkers ask "What?" They love to know facts and details and want to understand the reason that things work. They learn by thinking.

Inventor

- Wants to explore other possibilities
- Learns through innovation and implementation
- Asks What if?
- "Ah...ha..."
- Looks for how to implement
- Wants to improve and make it his/her own
- Seeks solutions

Inventors ask "What if?" They are never satisfied with the traditional use of information. They adjust the materials to fit their needs.

Driver

- Learns by doing
- Asks How?
- Uses common sense
- Likes risk
- Actively creates results
- Works step by step
- Is a problem solver
- Seeks to know how things work

Drivers ask "How?" Drivers want to try things out and actively create results. They learn by doing.

Why? · What? · What if? · How?

PAUL MITCHELL schools

Learning Strategy

Your learning strategy contains four areas. Discovering your preferences in each of these areas will assist you in planning a successful lifelong learning program:

Thinking process: Stringer and grouper
Receiving information: Visual, auditory, and kinesthetic
Processing and accessing information: Multiple intelligence
Applying and using information: Learning types

My Personal Learning Strategy

Fill in the boxes with your personal learning strategy.

Thinking Process	I am a…
Receiving Process	I prefer…
Processing and Assessing	My Multiple Intelligence is…
Using and Applying	I am a…

Learning is a verb and requires your participation and action. Learning is a skill that can be practiced and improved. Remember, what you learn is your responsibility.

How to Use The Color System

With **Paul Mitchell Schools The Color System**, *The Coloring Book,* DVD, and skill cards, you can create a personal learning program designed to involve all types of learners. In *The Coloring Book,* you will discover many questions, games, and activities to maximize your learning. Integrating your learning preferences will maximize your learning results.

With the DVD, you can customize your learning. You can view the DVD in sequence from beginning to end or you can jump around and watch it in any order you desire.

DVD Icons

Three different icons will pop up throughout the DVD: the head icon, the question mark icon, and the bottle icon.

Television viewing: Press "Enter" on your remote control when you see an icon appear.

Computer viewing: Click the cursor arrow directly on the icon.

The head icon indicates an interactive option to switch back and forth between a doll head and a live model. For optimal learning, allow 10 seconds to pass when switching back and forth.

The question mark icon indicates the option to discover a glossary term.

The bottle icon indicates the option to learn more about a Paul Mitchell color product.

Clicking on the return arrow will take you back to the previous menu or back to what you were previously viewing.

To navigate through the menu options, move the cursor up or down and then click "Enter" to select a menu option.

The Coloring Book Icons

Five different icons will appear throughout this book: the hand icon, the disc icon, the quality check icon, the circle arrow icon, and the skill card icon.

 The hand icon indicates an activity to perform to learn more.

 The disc icon indicates a section to view on the *The Color System* DVD.

 The quality check icon indicates a way to improve and check the quality of the work you do.

 The circle arrow icon reminds you to review the information to retain what you have learned.

 The skill card icon directs you to The Color System skill cards for product and tool options.

Disc One features the following menu options:

- *2 Ways to Color Hair*
- *Color Bar, featuring Robert Cromeans*
- *Extras*
- *Play All*
- *Credits*
- *Viewing Options*

In **2 Ways to Color Hair**, you will discover "All-Over Color and Foil Work" and "Shapes, Placement, and Effect."

You can also find under the **2 Ways to Color Hair** menu option:

- *Coloring and Lightening* — on live models and doll heads
- *Foil Work* — on live models and doll heads
- *Sectioning* — computer-graphic diagrams for each technique
- *Technique Key Points* — a review for each technique

Under **Extras**, you will find:

- *Rinsing and Shampooing* — how to properly rinse and shampoo color
- *Foil Preparation* — how to prepare your foils
- *Dropping Foils* — how to remove foils from the hair
- *SMA and Setup* — for proper organization
- *Adjusting Flaws* — how to fix color flaws
- *Locking* — how to "lock" a foil
- *Glossary* — words to know
- *Product* — features and benefits of Paul Mitchell color products
- *Trailer* — the fun color trailer to view
- *Hands-on Classes* — information for hands-on color classes

You can further customize your learning by clicking on **Viewing Options**, where you will discover seven listening options to enhance your auditory learning experience:

- Narration only
- Narration with up-tempo music
- Narration with chill-out music
- Narration with eclectic music
- Up-tempo music only
- Chill-out music only
- Eclectic music only

Disc Two features the following menu options:

- *Color Theory*
- *The Chemistry of Color*
- *The Interactive Color Map*
- *Extras*
  - Bonus feature: 5-Minute Makeup, 5-Minute Eye, 5-Minute Lip, 5-Minute Cheek, 5-Minute Review
- *Play All*
- *Credits*
- *Viewing Options*

The **Color Theory** menu option will explain:

- Laws of Color
- Light, Tone, and Depth

Measuring and Mixing will teach you how to properly measure and mix each of the Paul Mitchell color products.

To discover more about color theory, place **Disc Two** into your laptop or home computer and play with the Interactive Color Map. (See Chapter 6 for instructions on how to learn from the Interactive Color Map.)

Paul Mitchell Schools' *The Coloring Book*, *The Color System* DVD, and skill cards were designed to be used together. To enhance your learning and help you retain more information, use colored pencils or colored pens for note taking.

Who knew learning could be this *fun*…and so colorful! Enjoy!

The Color System

PAUL MITCHELL schools

Chapter 1
The Color Bar

The Experience

Build Loyalty

Creativity

Professionalism

Color Bar Success

The Color Bar^{sm}

Years ago people wanted to keep their hair coloring a secret to "just cover the gray." Not anymore! Now people are choosing bold beautiful colors and techniques that unleash their personalities and desires. As a hair colorist, your artistic creativity is unlimited. Maximizing the visual, hands-on use of The Color Bar provides an opportunity to convert any guest into a hair color lover, assuring the guest's chemical dependence upon you.

The Color Bar creates an experience that cannot be duplicated in the drugstore or at home by bringing color out of the back room and onto the service floor making it an *extraordinary color experience*. The Color Bar will effectively market your color services by involving the guest and spotlighting color services.

Benefits of The Color Bar include:

- Defense against drugstore or supermarket color
- Increased service revenue
- Visual merchandising that draws attention to color services
- Showcasing color service professionalism
- Involving the guest in the process
- Making hair color more exciting

The Color Bar is a fun and interactive way to educate and show guests how to upgrade their services in a language they can see and understand!

The Experience

The Color Bar is a unique experience that is exclusively available in Paul Mitchell schools and salons. It's an open-air color mixing area where you can celebrate hair color with your service guests. The Color Bar helps you to create a service experience that a service guest cannot replicate at home with over-the-counter hair color products.

The experience menu, at right, lists perfect pampering experiences in The Wash House^{sm}, dreamy color services, and a wide array of Take Home^{sm} options to style and finish any texture of hair, satisfying the most insatiable tastes.

Your Color Bar is more than a fixture; it is an opportunity to upgrade your guest's service into a customized experience. The true enemy to your business is drugstores and supermarkets. Take the opportunity in a fun and interactive way to invite your service guests to upgrade their services and involve them in The Color Bar experience, which is something they could not replicate at home.

Build Loyalty

Create excitement by sharing with your service guests the many creative possibilities you have to offer them at The Color Bar. By mixing three or four colors and involving them, you will create a fun and interactive way to educate and show them what is possible in hair color.

Master the service upgrade recommendation and offer The Color Bar experience to every one of your service guests and you will build awareness that will increase the number of hair color services you perform.

Finally, when you deliver beautiful and consistent hair color service results, you will build a loyal clientele who is willing to pay for your expertise.

Creativity

Use The Color Bar to channel your creativity. Explore the vast array of products featured at The Color Bar including Paul Mitchell® **the color**, PM SHINES®, The Blonding System, Color Shots®, and INKWORKS®. Take time to explore the products with your service guests and showcase your creativity. The best way to build creativity is to build your color knowledge. Use the DVD, book, and skill cards to help you master your color skills and knowledge. Then, allow your creativity to soar.

The Color Bar menu, at right, is part of the experience menu; it offers delicious, dreamy color services for any desiring guest.

Professionalism

Experience tours — Create an extraordinary experience by introducing The Color Bar to all new service guests as you provide them a tour of your school or salon.

Stage the experience — Prior to the service, make sure The Color Bar and service area are set and prepared for your service guest. Just like a fine dining experience, when you pay attention to details, your service guest will notice.

Be sure The Color Bar is clean and fully stocked, including bowls, brushes, and developers. Ensure your service area is ready and you have all of the tools, supplies, and materials needed to provide an extraordinary experience.

Provide a professional color consultation and service — Use The Color Bar menu to introduce color services during the service guest consultation. Showcase your color service professionalism by providing an expert color consultation and customized formula. From how you prepare for the service to formulation, mixing, and application, the service guest is involved in the process and can witness your expertise.

Color Bar Success

The Color Bar is a one-of-a-kind marketing tool that displays the Paul Mitchell color brand as alluring, eye candy that will spark your service guests' interest and questions. Once color was out of sight and locked away in the dispensary; now The Color Bar makes the color display area prime "real estate" in the salon or school designated for you to make color business happen.

The Color Bar shows beautifully racked and packed color with every tube aligned with displays of the developers, foils, color mixing bowls, and whisks. The color-coded packages, which show the shades and tonal base of each color, set side by side create a color wheel that a young colorist may view for the full spectrum of tones that the Paul Mitchell color line offers. The colors are beautifully coordinated using the level systems and colors to include INKWORKS, Paul Mitchell **the color**, PM SHINES, and The Blonding System. Sliding shelves or drawers hold the used tubes for mixing.

The only way to make your Color Bar work is to use it! The following activities will help you to better utilize this brilliant color-marketing tool.

Activity: Color Bar Guest Experience

Color Bar Image

What does your Color Bar look like?_____
_____

Is it clean and organized? What do you need to do to keep it clean and organized? _____
_____

Do you have bar seating?_____
_____

Do you have a *Color Bartender's Handbook*? _____
_____

Color Bar Service Marketing

How are you using your Color Bar menu as an effective service-marketing tool to drive color service sales?
_____

Is your clinic floor stocked with all of the color marketing tools?_____
_____

If not, where can you access the current color marketing tools? _____
_____

Color Bar Guest Experience

How can your team improve The Color Bar experience?_____
_____

What's working now? _____
_____

What needs to be refined?_____
_____

Activity: Making Your Color Bar Work!

Assess your Color Bar's effectiveness. Rate your Color Bar from 1 to 5:

❶ I'm not sure what a Color Bar is.

❷ We don't have a Color Bar yet.

❸ Our Color Bar is a beautiful piece of furniture, not fully used yet.

❹ Our Color Bar is utilized but needs better systems to improve profitability.

❺ Our Color Bar rocks! We have excellent sales and profitability!

Our Color Bar is beautifully branded with the most up-to-date marketing materials and Paul Mitchell professional hair color tools, products, and materials.

Not Yet ①——②——③——④——⑤ *Yes*

Our Color Bar is an effective service-marketing tool and it has improved our color service sales.

Not Yet ①——②——③——④——⑤ *Yes*

My team uses The Color Bar to create an extraordinary service experience for our service guests. *Explain how.*

Not Yet ①——②——③——④——⑤ *Yes*

Our Color Bar is profitable. We measure our profitability. *Explain how.*

Not Yet ①——②——③——④——⑤ *Yes*

We have a system to control product usage and waste. *Explain how.*

Not Yet ①——②——③——④——⑤ *Yes*

We manage inventory and theft. *Explain how.*

Not Yet ①——②——③——④——⑤ *Yes*

We use The Color Bar as an effective learning center.

Not Yet ①——②——③——④——⑤ *Yes*

We use our Color Bar to conduct hair color workshops or mini-classes.

Not Yet ①——②——③——④——⑤ *Yes*

Remember, you have the power to make sure your service guests are not taking it upon themselves to meet their hair color needs. It is your job to introduce your service guests to color and educate them about the endless possibilities. It is often said, *"A color client is a loyal client!"*

Remember these ideas:

- The Color Bar is a great defense against drugstore and supermarket color and it delivers a true experience.

- The Color Bar is a great example of visual merchandising and draws your guests' attention. When The Color Bar is kept clean and busy with activity, service guests become intrigued with the experience and ask questions about it. Their questions can be interpreted as buying signals; when they see others having great experiences, they let go of their fears about color.

- The Color Bar has increased color service revenue in salons and schools throughout the John Paul Mitchell Systems network.

- The Color Bar can become a profit center akin to the Take Home area. Think of every inch of your salon or school as real estate and an investment to build service revenue.

Watch and listen to "The Color Bar" on Disc One to fill in the blanks.

The Color Bar^{sm}

1. The Color Bar is a fixture. **True   False**
2. The Color Bar is a/an _____ of hair color.

The Experience

3. According to Robert, what is our true enemy? _____
   _____
   _____

4. How do we get clients or guests involved? _____
   _____
   _____

5. What do people truly want? _____
   _____
   _____

Loyalty

6. How do you build loyalty? _____
   _____

7. Clients and guests can create The Color Bar experience from supermarket color. **True   False**

Creativity

8. The Color Bar truly identifies the array of _____ that you have.
9. What can a drugstore never do? _____
   _____

Professionalism

10. What is Robert's definition of professionalism? _____
    _____

11. The main feature of The Color Bar is…
    A. To mix in front of a client or guest.   C. To see all of the amazing colors.
    B. To see all of the different steps.   D. All of the above.

Notes

Review

1. What is The Color Bar to you?
   _____
   _____

2. What additional elements would you add to The Color Bar?
   _____
   _____

3. How will you market The Color Bar?
   _____
   _____

4. What can you do to enhance the service guest's color experience?
   _____
   _____

5. What are some other ways you can create loyal service guests?
   _____
   _____

6. What do creativity and "mixing power" have in common?
   _____
   _____

7. What else can you do to prepare to become more professional?
   _____
   _____

8. What can you do to become a $500 colorist?
   _____
   _____

9. How does The Color Bar bring more revenue into a salon or school?
   _____
   _____

10. Where could you go to find more information on The Color Bar and the latest color marketing tools?
   _____
   _____

Activity

Using cardboard, foam core, color markers, pictures from a magazine, Popsicle sticks, and your own imagination, create a three-dimensional replica of a Color Bar.

Role-play giving a "tour" of The Color Bar with a partner by explaining the various color choices and how The Color Bar works.

Learning Review

Read

Check out the *Color Bartender's Handbook.*

Reflect

What did you learn about The Color Bar? How can you utilize The Color Bar in your services?

Review

Watch and listen to "The Color Bar" on Disc One and complete the questions in this chapter.

Select/Prioritize

With The Color Bar, identify what you will focus on to create a color experience for your service guests.

Draw

Design and draw what The Color Bar would look like in your dream salon.

Share/Act

Teach what you have learned to a friend or coworker.

The Color System

PAUL MITCHELL® schools

Chapter 2
Color Theory and Mixing

Chemistry and Hair Structure

Laws of Color

Light, Tone, and Depth

Formulation

Product Benefits, Features, Measuring, and Mixing

Color Removers

2 Ways to Color Hair

Color Theory and Mixing

Before beginning any color service, a great colorist must have a clear understanding of the many systems that create beautiful hair color. Successful hair coloring requires the understanding of color theory and the laws that govern hair coloring.

In this chapter, you will discover:

- Chemistry and hair structure
- Laws of color
- Light, tone, and depth and their visual effect on the color
- Color formulation
- Two ways to color hair
- Measuring and mixing color
- Understanding **the color** Map

The successful hair colorist must know these key factors to achieve the guest's desired results.

 Words to Remember

Before you begin, learn the key terms in this chapter. Locate the terms in the glossary.

Block Color	Gray coverage	Secondary colors
Cool	Incandescent light	Tertiary colors
Dominant pigment	Neutralize	Tone
Fluorescent light	Primary colors	Warm
Gray blending	Pure white light	"Whisper, Talk, Shout"

Chemistry and Hair Structure

Chemistry is an essential part of everything we do as future and salon professionals; however, many professionals lack the knowledge of the chemicals in products or the chemical reactions they create each day while working behind the chair.

Empowering future and salon professionals starts with a fundamental understanding of the chemical makeup of the products we use, as well as the basic structure of hair and how the coloring process affects it.

Human hair is a complex structure consisting of several components that each consist of several different chemical types. Hair is an integrated system in both its structure and its chemical and physical behavior.

The best colorists are not lucky; they are informed and knowledgeable.

 Watch and listen to "The Chemistry of Color" on Disc Two to complete the following activities.

1. What does *hydrophilic* mean? _____

2. How many layers of cuticle scale does fine hair have? _____

3. How many layers of cuticle scale does coarse hair have? _____

4. Label the parts of the hair structure.

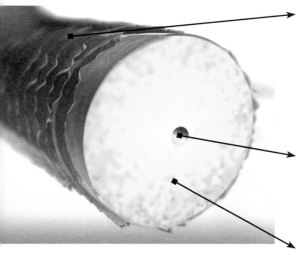

_____

- • _____ layer of the hair
- • Protects the _____ from _____ and _____ _____
- • Formed of _____, _____ scales
- • Has the ability to _____ and _____ as it _____ or _____ water

_____

- • _____ portion of the hair shaft
- • Composed of soft _____ _____ and _____ _____
- • No specific _____, _____, or _____

_____

- • _____ part of the hair
- • Represents approximately _____ percent of the total weight
- • Made of twisting fibers of _____ _____
- • Where the _____ resides

Chemical Makeup of Hair

5. Label the composition of human hair in the pie graph.

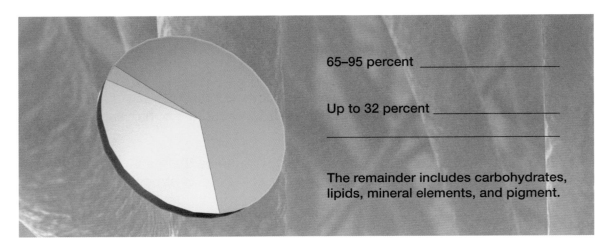

65–95 percent _____

Up to 32 percent _____

_____

The remainder includes carbohydrates, lipids, mineral elements, and pigment.

6. Match the following item to its function:

    Carbohydrates   Shine

    Lipids   Flexibility to the hair

    Minerals   Strength

7. How many amino acids are in the human body? _____
    How many relate to the hair? _____

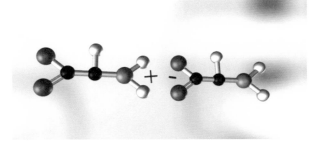

8. An amine tail is _____ and is represented by a _____ sign.

9. An acid head is _____ and is represented by a _____ sign.

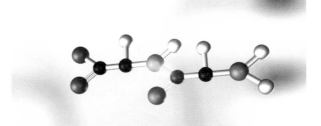

10. What is created when an acid head joins an amine tail? _____

11. Peptides link together to create a _____.
Multiple polypeptides create a _____
_____.

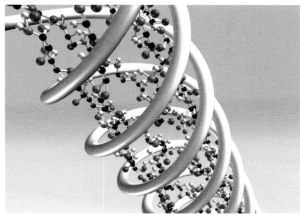

12. When a polypeptide chain has enough amino acids in it to equal multiple proteins, it is considered a/an _____.
A. Protein chain or helix coil
B. DNA chain
C. Atom chain or side bond

13. Polypeptide chains are cross-linked by covalent or _____ _____. They twist around each other to _____ a helical coil.

14. Approximately seven to nine of these helical coils twist and bind to form larger bundles called _____; then, twist again to form _____; and then twist once more to form fibrils or _____.
A. Micro fibrils; macro fibrils; cortical cells
B. Micro fibrils; cortical cells; macro fibrils
C. Macro fibrils; cortical cells; micro fibrils

15. Using the answers from #14, label the following images:

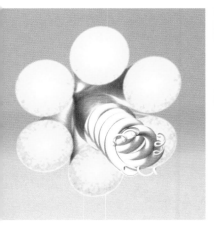

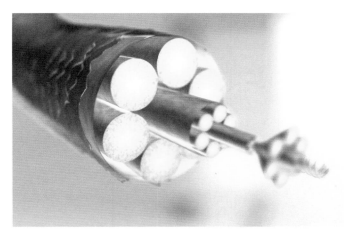

_____   _____   _____

16. Hydrogen bonds make up _____ of the hair's total strength.
    A. 65 percent
    B. One-third
    C. One-half

17. Hydrogen bonds are ionic and are easily affected by _____.
    A. Reactive chemicals
    B. Changes in pH
    C. Water and heat

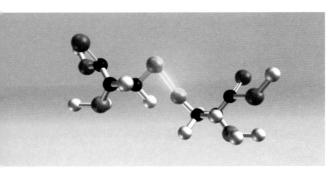

18. Salt bonds account for _____ of the hair's overall strength. Salt bonds are ionic, fairly weak, and affected by _____.
    A. One-half; reactive chemicals
    B. One-third; changes in pH
    C. One-third; water and heat

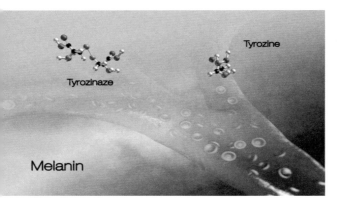

Tyrozine

Tyrozinaze

Melanin

19. Disulfide bonds are fewest in number, the strongest in the hair, and responsible for _____ of the structural strength. Disulfide bonds are affected by _____.
    A. One-third; reactive chemicals
    B. One-half; changes in pH
    C. One-third; water and heat

20. What are the three side bonds found in the hair?
    1. _____
    2. _____
    3. _____

Melanin

21. Melanocytes are specialized cells that create all of the melanin found in the
    _____, _____, and _____.

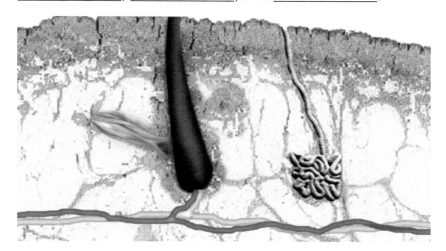

22. When hair begins to lose color or become gray, it is because the body no longer
    produces the necessary quantities of _____ _____ to promote the
    production of _____.

23. When production stops completely, the hair becomes _____.
    A. More gray
    B. Silver/gray
    C. Silver
    D. White

24. Match the characteristics to the two types of melanin.

	Levels 1–5
	Oxidation turns red
Eumelanin	Levels 6 and higher
	Black to brown in color
	Reddish orange in color
Pheomelanin	Contains copper
	Oxidation turns orange
	Contains more iron

Basic Chemistry

25. An ion is a _____ with an _____ charge.

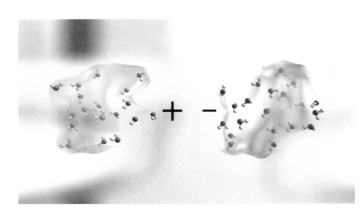

26. When a molecule ionizes, it _____ into two parts, creating a pair of ions with opposite _____ charges.

27. The ion with a _____ charge is called a hydrogen ion, which is _____.

28. The ion with a _____ charge is called a hydroxide ion, which is _____.

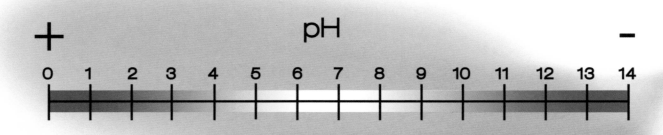

Note: You can learn more about pH in the ABCD's of Hair Color.

29. pH is only present where there is _____.

30. pH stands for _____ _____, which means the _____ ___ _____.

31. The pH scale is a measurement of acidic and alkaline ions. **True   False**

32. When the amount of positive and negative ions is equal, the pH is _____ on the pH scale.
    A. Less damaging
    B. Neutral or 7
    C. More damaging

33. The pH scale ranges from zero to 14 and is _____, which means that moving either way on the pH scale results in a _____ increase in the degree of alkalinity or acidity.
    A. Logarithmic; tenfold
    B. Mathematical; hundredfold
    C. Exponential; thousandfold

34. Match the item with its proper pH on the scale.

pH Scale

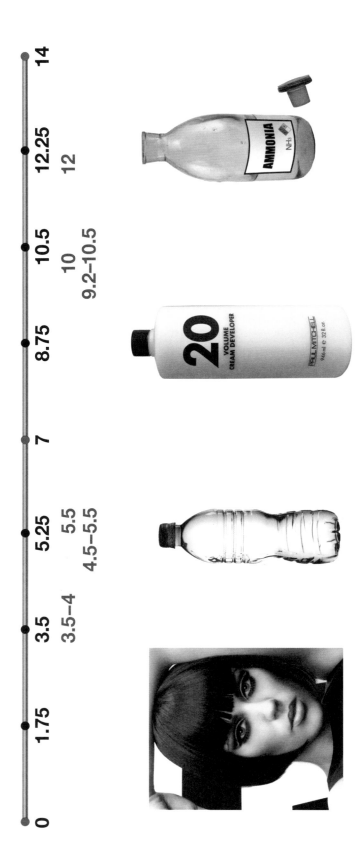

0	1.75	3.5	5.25	7	8.75	10.5	12.25	14
		3.5–4	5.5			10	12	
			4.5–5.5			9.2–10.5		

Classifications of Hair Color

35. Match the hair color classifications with their definitions.

Semi-permanent

Demi-permanent

Permanent

Dye molecules sit on the outside of the hair

Lasts six to eight weeks

Produces lift

Lasts two to three weeks

Dye molecules penetrate the cuticle without lifting

Does not penetrate into the cuticle

Oxidative dyes

Displaces melanin

36. Permanent hair colors are generally marketed as two separate components.

One component contains the dye precursors and _____ in an alkaline base.

The other component is a stabilized solution of _____ _____.

 =

Ammonia

37. Ammonia is _____ and raises the pH of hair by removing
_____ _____, which leaves the hair in an _____ state.

38. Two _____ ions will repel each other just like two _____ _____ of a magnet.

39. This makes the hair swell and separates the cortical cells causing what we know as _____.

   A. Density

   B. Porosity

   C. Elasticity

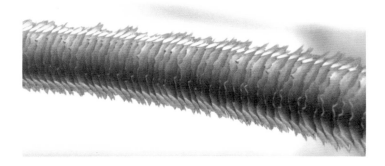

Hydrogen Peroxide

40. One vital and often misunderstood ingredient used in creating artificial hair color is _____ _____, which is a combination of _____ and _____. When mixed with ammonia, it generates _____.

   A. Metallic dyes; water and hydrogen; neutralization

   B. Hydrogen peroxide; water and oxygen; oxidation

   C. Vegetable henna; oxygen and pigments; energy

41. The volume of hydrogen peroxide varies and is chosen for its ability to _____.

   A. Control lift and coverage

   B. Deposit and cover gray hair

   C. Lift and monitor color

42–43. Fill in percentage and volume strength.

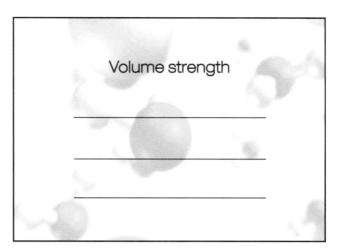

Percentage strength

_____

_____

_____

Volume strength

_____

_____

_____

44. List the percentages under each volume.

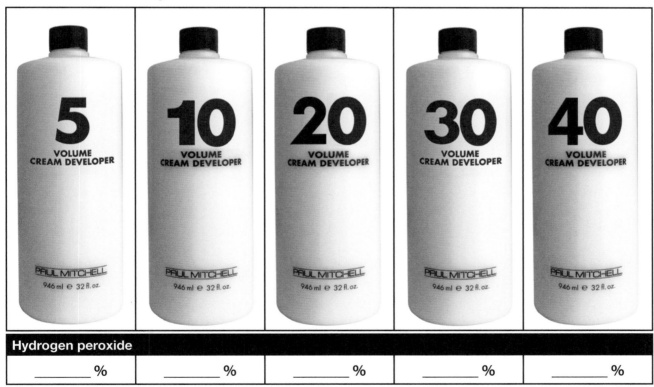

Hydrogen peroxide				
_____ %	_____ %	_____ %	_____ %	_____ %

Chemistry of Lightening

45. The most effective lightener is _____ _____.

46. Lightening agents are made of two basic parts. Match the following:

Oxidizing agent

Breaks down the hydrogen peroxide
Acts as a catalyst

Alkaline substance

Hydrogen peroxide
Provides oxygen for lightening
Releases the oxygen

47. During the lightening process, the _____ and _____ in the cortex is _____ to colorless compounds.

48. The goal of lightening hair with lightener is to oxidize the melanin with as little oxidation of the bonds as possible to _____.
   A. Make the hair as light as possible
   B. Minimize damage to the hair
   C. Lighten and deposit in one step

 Activity: Hair Structure

Using straws, Tinkertoys, construction paper, plastic or rubber tubing, Styrofoam balls, pipe cleaners, or whatever else you can find, create a hair structure to include atoms, amino acids, polypeptide chains, helix coil, micro fibril, macro fibril, and cortical cell.

pH

Purchase litmus paper from a pharmacy, pool supply, or fish aquarium store. Gather liquid products that contain water such as shampoos, conditioners, hydrogen peroxide, hair color, relaxers, perms, lighteners, etc. Test each product with the litmus paper and record your findings.

Laws of Color

Color is life and life is color! Understanding and comprehending color as it relates to everyday life can open doors to the world of hair color. To study color is to study life.

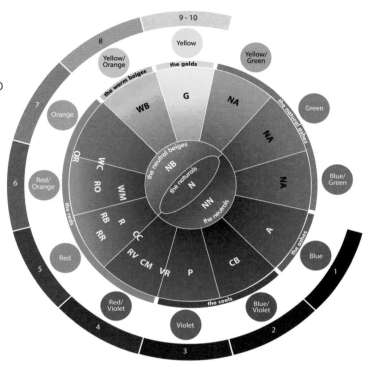

 Watch and listen to "Laws of Color" on Disc Two to answer the following questions.

1. What is an example of a true law? _____
_____
_____
_____

2. Are the laws of color a true law? **Yes   No**

3. Primary colors are colors that cannot be made by mixing other colors.
True   False

4. The primary colors are _____, _____,
and _____.

5. Secondary colors are created when two or more primary colors are combined in equal parts. **True   False**

Notes
_____
_____
_____
_____
_____
_____
_____
_____
_____
_____
_____
_____
_____
_____

6. Secondary colors are _____, _____, and _____.

7. Tertiary colors are created when a _____ and a _____ color are combined in equal parts.

8. The tertiary colors are _____, _____, _____, _____, _____, and _____.

9. All primary colors mixed together in equal parts create _____.

   A. A neutral color
   B. Black
   C. A rainbow
   D. A colored prism

10. To control or cancel dominant pigment means that you want to neutralize an unwanted color result. **True   False**

11. To control or cancel dominant pigment, you move _____.

   A. Directly to the next color on the Paul Mitchell **the color** Map
   B. Directly across the Paul Mitchell **the color** Map
   C. Perpendicular on the Paul Mitchell **the color** Map
   D. Around the Paul Mitchell **the color** Map

12. To cancel out yellow in the hair, the two missing primary colors are _____ and _____.

   A. Red, orange
   B. Blue, green
   C. Red, blue
   D. Blue, more yellow

Light, Tone, and Depth

It's all about lighting! The right light can make hair and skin tones look healthy and attractive, whereas the wrong light can make hair and skin tones look greenish and pale.

Understanding lighting and its effect on coloring hair will assist you in creating the proper color formulation for extraordinary color results.

Incandescent light, fluorescent light, and natural light sources will affect colors in the hair and on skin tones differently.

 Watch and listen to "Light, Tone, and Depth" on Disc Two to answer the following questions.

1. Identify the type of light shown in each picture.

_____   _____   _____

2. Incandescent light comes from a regular light bulb and favors _____, so it gives a warm reflection against the hair and skin.
    A. Cool tones
    B. Warm tones
    C. Orange tones
    D. True tones

3. Fluorescent lighting has a diffusing capability that reduces _____ and spreads _____.

4. Fluorescent lighting highlights _____ on the hair and skin.
   A. Split ends and wrinkles
   B. Dullness and blemishes
   C. Cool tones
   D. Neutral tones

5. Pure white light or natural light gives the truest tone. **True   False**

6. Without light, there is no _____.
   A. Reflection
   B. Sunshine
   C. Tanning
   D. Color

Activity

Go to your local hardware store and purchase three inexpensive (under $10) clamp lights and three light bulbs: one warm (halogen) bulb, one cool (fluorescent) bulb, and one natural (plant grow light) light bulb. Take turns having one person and then the other sit at the service area. Cover their body with a black cape and drape a white cloth across their chest to reflect the light. Have them face the mirror as you shine each light, one by one, on their face and hair. Observe how the warm light, cool light, and natural light affect each person's skin tones and hair color.

Do you see more or fewer wrinkles?
Do you see more or fewer dark circles under their eyes?
Does their skin look too warm or too cool?
Do they look healthy or anemic?
Which light makes their skin tone and hair color look the best?
Does their hair color look dull and flat or does it look shiny and bright?

Next, go outside — in the mid-morning or mid-afternoon is best — and look at each other's skin tones and hair color.

What do you see?
What has improved or looks better?
How does their skin tone look better?
How does their hair color look better?

1. How does understanding light, tone, and depth improve color consultations?

    _____

    _____

    _____

    _____

    _____

2. Why is it important to learn about proper lighting?

    _____

    _____

    _____

    _____

    _____

3. What else can you learn about lighting?

    _____

    _____

    _____

    _____

    _____

4. Match the lights to the occasion.

    Red and green lights   Summer

    Candlelight   Halloween

    Red, pink, and white lights   Romantic nights

    Sunlight   Christmas

    Orange and black lights   Valentine's Day

Formulation

Knowing how to formulate properly and to consider the many factors that affect beautiful hair color are the keys to becoming a successful colorist. Formulation is your travel guide to a fantastic color experience. To achieve the optimum end results, you must follow proper formulation steps. Factors that you will want to consider when formulating are natural level, canvas level or previous color, desired level and tonal base, and the dominant pigment at the desired level.

Paul Mitchell **the color** Map

Understanding the laws of color and the Paul Mitchell **the color** Map will allow you to create the desired outcome of your color service through proper formulation. Paul Mitchell **the color** Map is based on the laws of color theory. Primary, secondary, and tertiary colors mixed in the proper combination following the laws of color will produce beautiful results.

Activity
Fill in **the color** Map.

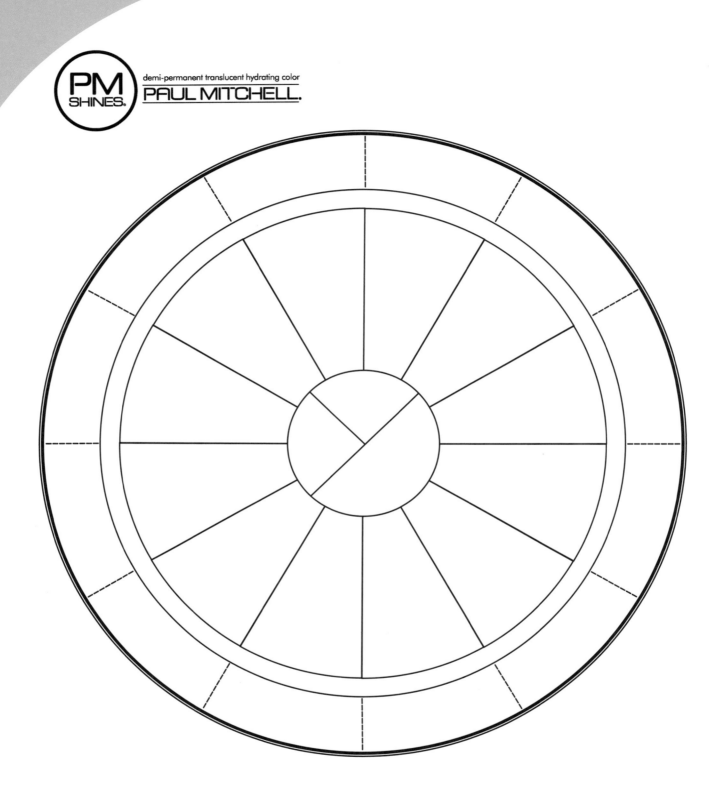

demi-permanent translucent hydrating color
PAUL MITCHELL.

Activity
Fill in the PM SHINES Color Map.

Formulation Guidelines

Formulation Steps

1

1. Determine the natural level/percentage of gray.
2. Identify the target level.
3. Determine the dominant pigment at the target level.
4. Refer to the Color Map to determine how to neutralize or intensify the pigment.

Pigment Chart

Level	Shade Name	Dominant Pigment	Neutralizing Base
10	LIGHTEST BLONDE	PALE YELLOW	Violet
9	VERY LIGHT BLONDE	YELLOW	Violet
8	LIGHT BLONDE	YELLOW/ ORANGE	Blue/Violet
7	BLONDE	ORANGE	Blue
6	DARK BLONDE	RED/ ORANGE	Blue/Green
5	LIGHT BROWN	RED	Green
4	BROWN	RED/ VIOLET	Yellow/Green
3	DARK BROWN	VIOLET	
2	DARKEST BROWN	BLUE/ VIOLET	
1	BLACK	BLUE	

Gray Coverage

2

% of Gray	
25% – 50%	1:3 – 1:2 (N, NB or NN with selected shade)
50% – 75%	1:2 – 1:1 (N, NB or NN with selected shade)
75% – 100%	1:1 – 2:1 (N, NB or NN with selected shade)

*The mixing ratios above are based on parts. For example, 1:3 = 1 part N and 3 parts R.

Formulating with Paul Mitchell® the color Map

3

Use Paul Mitchell **the color** Map and the tonal chart below to determine what tonal series to use to neutralize or intensify.

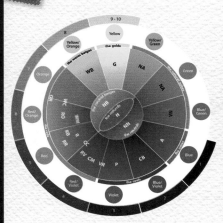

Tonal Bases

NN	gray/brown
N	natural brown
NB	neutral beige

NA	green with brown
CB	beige with blue/violet
CM	violet/red with brown
RB	red with brown
WM	red/orange with brown
WB	beige with yellow/orange
RV	red/violet
CC	natural red/violet
R	red
RO	red/orange
WC	natural orange/red
G	yellow/gold
A	gray/blue
P	violet
VR	violet/red
RR	red/red
OR	orange/red

Tonal Result Guidelines

To neutralize
Go across the Color Map and choose the tone that is opposite the dominant pigment tone at the target level.

To intensify
Choose tones that are near or the same as the dominant pigment tone at the target level.

Consider using Color Shots® to neutralize or intensify.

Processing

4

	Uses	Mixing and Processing	Timing with or w/o Color Shots
PERMANENT	1 to 2 levels of lift or deposit + gray coverage	20 volume Developer on dry hair	35 minutes
	2 to 3 levels of lift	30 volume Developer on dry hair	35 minutes
	3 levels of lift	40 volume Developer on dry hair	35 minutes
HIGHLIFTS	4 levels of lift	double 40 volume Cream Developer on dry hair	45 minutes
	4 levels of lift with more tone	40 volume Cream Developer on dry hair	45 minutes
DEMI-PERMANENT LONGEVITY 4-6 WEEKS	deposit only + gray blending	5 volume Developer on damp hair	20 minutes
SEMI-PERMANENT LONGEVITY UP TO 3 WEEKS	deposit only + minimal gray blending	10 volume Developer on damp hair	10 minutes
ULTRA TONERS	deposit only	5 volume Developer on damp hair, check color development for desired tone at 10 minutes	10-20 minutes

Technical Support:

877.610.5405 (within North America)

01296.390.544 (within the United Kingdom)

1300.365.350 (within Australia)

REPIGMENTATION FORMULATION STEPS

When depositing more than two levels on previously lightened or processed/damaged hair, repigmentation is recommended. Before you begin, refer to the pre-treatment chart in the Fabric section to identify specific products for processed or damaged hair.

1. Identify the target level of desired end result.
2. Select the proper target level repigmentation formula below.
3. Mix the repigmentation formula with equal parts 10-volume Developer and apply to damp hair.
4. Process for a minimum of 10 minutes.
5. Mix and apply the target formula directly over the repigmentation formula. If the target color is cool or neutral, wipe off the repigmentation formula.
6. Process for an additional 35 minutes.

REPIGMENTATION FORMULAS

Target level 8: 2 parts 10G and 1 part 8RO with 10-volume Developer
Target level 7: Equal parts 10G and 8RO with 10-volume Developer
Target level 6: 8RO with 10-volume Developer
Target level 5: Equal parts 6RO and 8R with 10-volume Developer
Target level 4: Equal parts 6R and 6RO with 10-volume Developer

FABRIC

The quality of the final result depends on the condition of the hair with which you start. For the best color results, you may need to pre-condition the hair prior to applying Paul Mitchell **the color**.

Follow this system to determine the condition of the hair.
Rate the hair in the following three categories: elasticity, porosity, and texture.

PRE-TREATMENT CHART

HAIR TYPE	PRE-COLOR
Virgin/Healthy	Shampoo Two® Awapuhi Moisture Mist®
Normal-to-Dry	Shampoo Two® Super-Charged Moisturizer®
Chemically-treated to Damaged	Shampoo Three® Hair Repair Treatment® or Super Strong® Treatment

For elasticity and porosity, grade the hair in the following manner:

Virgin/Healthy = 1

Normal/Dry = 2

Processed/Damaged = 3

For texture, grade the hair in this manner:

Fine = 1

Medium = 2

Coarse = 3

Example:

Your guest's hair:

Elasticity — virgin/healthy = 1

Porosity — normal/dry = 2

Texture — fine = 1

Total = 4

Once you have graded each area, add all three together to total one final score. Find the final score below to determine the hair's overall condition.

| 3 = Virgin/Healthy | 4-5-6 = Normal/Dry | 7-8-9 = Processed/Damaged |

Use the pre-treatment chart to find the recommended Paul Mitchell products to care for that hair type before the Paul Mitchell **the color** service.

COLOR BALANCING PREVIOUSLY COLORED HAIR

When coloring previously colored hair, be aware that other hair color products may have progressive or undeveloped dye molecules; this means the old color may begin processing again. Because hair color products are unable to lift artificial hair color, color balancing is recommended prior to the first application of Paul Mitchell **the color**. Apply to previously tinted hair only.

Directions:
- Mix equal parts of Paul Mitchell Shampoo One®, 10-volume Cream Developer, and Dual-Purpose Lightener.
- Apply to wet hair and emulsify until the slightest change in the previous color is seen.
- Process approximately 5–10 minutes. Rinse thoroughly and shampoo with Color Protect® Post Color Shampoo.

MIXING

1. Always mix Paul Mitchell **the color** levels 1–10 and the Ultra Toners with Cream or Clear Developer in equal parts (1:1 ratio).
2. If using Color Shots®, add Color Shots after the color is mixed with Developer.

APPLICATION

Virgin application going lighter
1. Section the hair into four quadrants.
2. Apply color ½ inch from the scalp to the point where the ends show damage or porosity.
3. Process for 10 minutes.
4. Remix and apply color to the root area and then to the ends.
5. Process for 35 minutes for permanent results.

Virgin application same level or darker
1. Section the hair into four quadrants.
2. Apply color from scalp to ends.*
3. Process for 35 minutes for permanent results.
   *If extreme porosity is present, pre-treatment is recommended (see pre-treatment chart). Color balancing is recommended prior to the first application of Paul Mitchell **the color** (see color balancing).

Retouch application steps
1. Apply the chosen formula to new growth.
2. Refresh the mid-shaft and ends with the chosen formula of Paul Mitchell **the color** or PM SHINES® and process appropriately.

HIGHIFT SERIES MIXING AND APPLICATION

For maximum lift
Mix the Highlift Series with Cream Developer only (1:2 ratio)

For a more toned end result
Mix the Highlift Series with Cream Developer only (1:1 ratio)

Virgin Application
1. Section the hair into four quadrants.
2. Apply color ½ inch from the scalp to the point where the ends show damage or porosity.
3. Process for 20 minutes.
4. Remix and apply color to the root area and then to the ends.
5. Process for an additional 45 minutes.

Retouch Application
1. Section the hair into four quadrants.
2. Apply color to regrowth only.
3. Process for 45 minutes.
4. To refresh faded ends, color may be worked through for the last 5–10 minutes.

COLOR RINSING AND POST CARE

After color processing is complete, rinse color thoroughly out of the hair and follow with Color Protect® Post Color Shampoo and Color Protect® Daily Conditioner. Recommend that guests use Paul Mitchell Color Care products to maintain the color at home.

The Blonding System

Creating beautiful blondes is easy with the right tools. The Blonding System from Paul Mitchell professional hair color provides an out-of-the-box lightening experience with brilliant, healthy-looking results. Formulating on fragile hair? Reach for Lighten Up®, the gentle choice for on- and off-scalp lightening. Need added power? Try Dual-Purpose Lightener for added lift with control. Expand your options even further and use The Blonding System with Flash Finish®, PM SHINES®, and Paul Mitchell® **the color** Highlift Series and Ultra Toners for a world of creative options.

PIGMENT CHART

Level	Shade Name	Dominant Pigment		Neutralizing Base
10	LIGHTEST BLONDE	PALE YELLOW		Violet
9	VERY LIGHT BLONDE	YELLOW		Violet
8	LIGHT BLONDE	YELLOW/ORANGE		Blue/Violet
7	BLONDE	ORANGE		Blue
6	DARK BLONDE	RED/ORANGE		Blue/Green
5	LIGHT BROWN	RED		Green
4	BROWN	RED/VIOLET		Yellow/Green
3	DARK BROWN	VIOLET		
2	DARKEST BROWN	BLUE/VIOLET		
1	BLACK	BLUE		

STEPS TO SUCCESSFUL LIGHTENING

1. Determine desired end result (level and tone).

2. Choose the appropriate lightening product, Paul Mitchell **the color** Highlift Series, Lighten Up or Dual-Purpose Lightener (based on levels of lift, fabric and texture).

3. Determine the dominant pigment at the desired level.

4. Pre-lighten to the desired level.

5. Finish with Flash Finish, PM SHINES or Paul Mitchell **the color** Ultra Toners (if needed).

6. Shampoo and finish with the appropriate Paul Mitchell conditioner or treatment.

Seven Stages of Lightening

7th Pale Yellow	7
6th Yellow	6
5th Yellow/Gold	5
4th Orange/Yellow	4
3rd Orange	3
2nd Red/Orange	2
1st Red	1

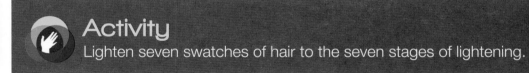

Activity

Lighten seven swatches of hair to the seven stages of lightening.

ABCD's of Hair Color

Before you begin, learn the following terms. Locate the terms in the glossary.

A = Ammonia

_____

_____

B = Base

_____

_____

C = Color Pigment

_____

_____

Color Chemistry: The two types of dyes most commonly used in hair color are:

• Oxidative Dyes   _____

• Direct Dyes   _____

Hair coloring products use dye intermediates to color hair. The selected hair color type, developer, and processing time will determine whether the color is semi-permanent, demi-permanent, or permanent. (ABC's live in the tube or bottle of hair color.)

D = Developer (or H_2O_2)   _____

_____

The pH scale ranges from 0–14. A pH of 7 indicates a neutral solution; a pH below 7 indicates an acidic solution; and a pH above 7 indicates an alkaline solution. Solutions that are acidic contract and harden the hair and alkaline solutions soften and swell the hair.

The pH scale is a logarithmic scale, which means multiples of 10 or a change of one whole number represents a tenfold change in pH. For example, a pH of 8 is 10 times more alkaline than a pH of 7. A change of two whole numbers represents a change of 10 times 10, or a hundredfold change, which means that a pH of 9 is 100 times more alkaline than a pH of 7.

Alkalinity increases as the pH number increases and decreases as the pH number decreases, which means that a higher pH (greater number) is more alkaline than a lower pH number. For example, 9 is more alkaline than 8; 10 is more alkaline than 9; and so on. On the other side of the scale, acidity increases as the pH number decreases, which means that a lower pH (lesser number) is more acidic than a higher pH number. For example, 5 is more acidic than 6; 4 is more acidic than 5; and so on.

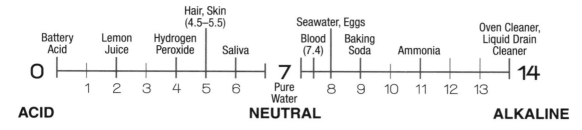

pH Scale (Potential Hydrogen)

Battery Acid — Lemon Juice — Hydrogen Peroxide — Hair, Skin (4.5–5.5) — Saliva — Blood (7.4) — Seawater, Eggs — Baking Soda — Ammonia — Oven Cleaner, Liquid Drain Cleaner

0 1 2 3 4 5 6 7 Pure Water 8 9 10 11 12 13 14

ACID   **NEUTRAL**   **ALKALINE**

ACID	ALKALINE
Generally closes the cuticle H_2O_2 = Developer (D)	Generally opens the cuticle Color = ABC's

$$D + ABC = Color$$

(acid)   (alkaline)

Professional Color Terminology

Professional color has been simplified by the use of the universal numbering system. Color levels are identified by a number that represents the level of depth from lightest to darkest. The tone is represented by a letter that refers to the color or shade chosen, such as a red brown (red being the tonal value). The following chart refers to both but also includes a dominant pigment chart and the corrective base that would be used to neutralize unwanted tones as needed. When formulating with Paul Mitchell **the color**, the most important factor to determine is the desired percentage of natural pigment you want reflected in the end result. It is easy to predict. Your color formulation will determine if the color is neutralized, intensified, or enhanced.

Read and review **the color** Map and swatch guide to fill in the blanks on the following pages.

LEVEL	DOMINANT PIGMENT	CORRECTIVE BASE
10 Lightest blonde		
9 Light blonde		
8 Medium blonde		
7 Blonde		
6 Darkest blonde		
5 Light brown		
4 Medium brown		
3 Brown		
2 Darkest brown		
1 Black		

TONAL BASE CHART

NN	gray/brown
N	
NB	
NA	
CB	
CM	
RB	
WM	
WB	
A	
P	
VR	
RV	
CC	
RR	
R	
RO	
WC	
OR	
G	

N. E. I.

When formulating, Step 4 of the blueprint for formulation is to determine the tonal result desired. Based on the desired end result, you either neutralize unwanted tone, continue by going lighter, or intensify by adding the natural dominant pigment tone. Refer to "Whisper, Talk, Shout."

Neutralize _____

_____

_____

Enhance _____

_____

_____

Intensify _____

_____

_____

Developer/H$_2$O$_2$

Choosing level and tone in a color formulation is not a complicated task but must be done with thought and planning. Formulation becomes clearer and is done with two major facts in mind.

❶ Hair coloring products can lift and deposit color into the hair (as discussed previously with level and tone).

❷ The volume of hydrogen peroxide lifts or lightens the natural color of the hair and develops the artificial pigment.

When mixed together in the proper level and strength, artificial hair color and hydrogen peroxide will provide both lift and/or deposit.

Energy allows the H$_2$O$_2$ to perform its job of oxidizing pigment (consuming it); then, the energy drives the color molecules inside the hair shaft on higher volumes or to lie on the outer cuticle on lower volumes. You choose the energy based on the desired result.

H$_2$O$_2$	USES
5 Volume:	
10 Volume:	
20 Volume:	
30 Volume:	
40 Volume:	

Formulation

1 — Formulation Steps

1. _____
2. _____
3. _____
4. _____

2 — Gray Coverage

Percentage of Gray	
25% – 50%	
50% – 75%	
75% – 100%	

3 — Formulating with Paul Mitchell *the color* Map

Tonal result guidelines

To neutralize _____

_____

To intensify _____

_____

4 — Processing

	Uses	Mixing and Processing	Timing With or Without Color Shots
Permanent			
Highlifts			
Demi-permanent *Longevity: Four to six weeks*			
Semi-permanent *Longevity: Up to three weeks*			
Ultra Toners			

Product Benefits, Features, Measuring, and Mixing

Proper measuring and mixing is essential not only for achieving consistent results but for the success of the overall color. Following the manufacturer's recommended measuring and mixing instructions is vital for your safety and for the safety of your guests.

On Disc One, click on the "bottle" icon or go to the Product menu to learn more about Paul Mitchell color and lightening products. Fill in the benefits and features of the products in the space provided on the following pages.

Watch and listen to "Measuring and Mixing" on Disc Two to learn which developers to use as well as how to measure and mix each product. Write the measuring information in the space provided on the following pages.

Dual-Purpose Lightener

Paul Mitchell Dual-Purpose Lightener is a powder that can be used for on- and off-scalp applications. It lifts hair fast and evenly with control. Natural oils of jojoba and castor bean, in a unique encapsulation process, buffer the lightening process to reduce damage and replenish lost nutrients. Paul Mitchell Dual-Purpose Lightener is a dust-free formula that provides a safe and pleasant working environment. The sandalwood fragrance offers a soothing guest experience.

Benefits

- Dual purpose _____

  _____

- Controlled, even lift _____

  _____

- Soothing fragrance _____

  _____

Features

- Conditioning and soothing _____

  _____

- Safe and pleasant _____

- Dual-purpose application _____

  _____

How to Measure

- Measure _____

  _____

- On-scalp application _____

  _____

- Off-scalp application _____

  _____

Tips for Mixing Dual-Purpose Lightener

- Remove the scoop from the container and close the lid.
- Shake the container to evenly disperse the conditioning oils.
- Scoop Dual-Purpose Lightener and pour into a bowl.
- Whisk the dry powder in the bowl using the mixing whisk to remove any lumps.
- Measure the appropriate amount of Cream Developer.
- Gradually add the developer to the lightener and continue mixing with a whisk or brush until you have a creamy texture.
- Processing time will vary depending on the desired level of lift and the condition of the hair.
- Heat is not recommended.

Lighten Up®

Create beautiful, natural-looking blonde hues with Lighten Up blonding paste, the gentle choice for on- and off-scalp blonding. Lift up to five levels quickly and easily thanks to specially balanced lifting agents. A unique combination of conditioners helps prevent moisture loss and reduce damage, while soothing aloe helps minimize scalp irritation for a comfortable lightening experience. Designed for use with 5, 10, 20, 30, and 40-volume Cream or Clear Developer, Lighten Up's beeswax base offers a smooth consistency for a controlled, flexible application and reliably brilliant results.

Benefits
- Rapid lift _____
  _____
- Gentle on the hair and scalp _____
  _____
- Smooth consistency _____
  _____

Features
- Conditioning and soothing_____
  _____
- Non-irritating _____
  _____
- Dual application_____
  _____

How to Measure

- On-scalp application_____
  _____

- Off-scalp application_____
  _____

- Place the key in the end of the Lighten Up tube and turn to dispense the product into the bowl.
- Gradually add the developer and mix with a whisk or brush; continue mixing until you have a fluffy texture.
- Processing time will vary depending on the desired level of lift and condition of the hair.
- The maximum timing is 50 minutes.
- Heat is not recommended.

Ultra Toners

The Ultra Toners are used to neutralize, enhance, or intensify highlighted or pre-lightened hair.

- **Long-lasting pastel tones** — Low ammonia, demi-permanent color in five tonal bases
- **Healthy, natural-looking blondes** — Beeswax base and natural conditioners
- **Eucalyptus fragrance** — Offers guests a pleasant hair coloring experience

Tips for Mixing Ultra Toners

Measure 1.5 oz or 45 ml of **the color** Ultra Toners with 1.5 oz or 45 ml of 5-volume Developer on damp hair and process for 10–20 minutes.

The Ultra Toners are available in five intermixable tonal bases — P, N, NB, G, and A — that provide long-lasting pastel tones:

Ultra Toner (P) — Platinum Blonde

Ultra Toner (N) — Natural Blonde

Ultra Toner (NB) — Neutral Blonde

Ultra Toner (G) — Gold Blonde

Ultra Toner (A) — Ash Blonde

Flash Finish®
Sheer Rapid Toner

Create the perfect icing on any blonde confection, in The Wash House or at The Color Bar. Flash Finish sheer rapid toner creates an ideal tone in under 10 minutes — it's fast, easy, and conditioning. Five sheer, lustrous shades allow you to neutralize, enhance, warm up, or cool down lightened locks in a flash.

Benefits

• Sheer, subtle tones _____
_____
_____

• Tones _____
_____
_____

• Adds shine and condition _____
_____
_____

Features

• Liquid gel _____
_____

• Pure tone _____
_____

• No lift _____
_____

• Imparts shine _____
_____

• Available _____
_____

• Fresh _____
_____

How to Measure

• Measure _____
_____

- Measure 5-volume Cream or Clear Developer into the beaker or applicator bottle.
- Open the bottle and add Flash Finish to the beaker or applicator bottle.
- If using a bowl-and-brush application, pour the contents of the beaker into the mixing bowl. Use a brush or mixing whisk to mix the color into a gel-like consistency.
- If using an applicator-bottle application, place the lid on the bottle. Slightly squeeze the bottle, cover the tip of the bottle with your finger, and shake the mixture into a gel-like consistency.

Paul Mitchell® the color

Paul Mitchell **the color** is a low-ammonia, permanent cream hair color that can be used as a permanent, demi-permanent, or semi-permanent hair color.

Paul Mitchell **the color** has ChromaLuxe™ technology, which means greater performance and easier mixing. ChromaLuxe technology provides:

- **Increased vibrancy** — An improved delivery system featuring new dyes and dye combinations offers better vibrancy and longer-lasting color.
- **Enhanced condition and shine** — Hair looks and feels more manageable with improved condition and shine.
- **Creamier consistency** — Same great beeswax base, now with a smoother consistency that's easier to mix and apply.

Benefits

- Outstanding _____
  _____
  _____

- Full spectrum_____
  _____
  _____

- Low cost _____
  _____
  _____

Features

- Low ammonia _____
  _____

- Natural beeswax base _____
  _____

- Advanced oxidative dyes _____
  _____

- ChromaLuxe™ technology _____
  _____

How to Measure

- Measure _____
  _____
  _____

- Color Shots
  Add _____
  _____
  _____
  Add _____
  _____
  _____

Tips for Mixing the color

- Place the key in the end of the tube and turn to dispense the product into the bowl.
- Use the side of the color tube to measure and dispense the color into a mixing bowl.
- For easier mixing, begin to whisk Paul Mitchell **the color** using a mixing whisk before adding the developer.
- Pour the appropriate developer into a measuring beaker.
- Gradually add the developer into the bowl and mix.
- Continue mixing until you have added all of the developer.
- Mix into a creamy consistency.

Paul Mitchell® *the color* Highlift Series

The Highlift Series is a low-ammonia, permanent cream hair color with a beeswax base. It consists of five intermixable colors.

Benefits and Features

- Maximum lift _____

  _____

- Long-lasting tonal control _____

  _____

- Sandalwood fragrance _____

  _____

- Lift and control _____

  _____

How to Measure

- 1:1 — Measure _____

  _____

- 1:2 — Measure _____

  _____

Tips for Mixing *the color* Highlift Series

- Place the key in the end of the tube and turn to dispense the product into the bowl.
- Use the side of the color tube to measure and dispense the color into a mixing bowl.
- For easier mixing, begin to whisk Paul Mitchell **the color** using a mixing whisk before adding the developer.
- Pour the appropriate developer into a measuring beaker.
- Gradually add the developer into the bowl and mix.
- Continue mixing until you have added all of the developer.
- Mix into a creamy consistency.

PM SHINES®

PM SHINES — a deposit-only, ammonia-free, demi-permanent hair color — features our exclusive Intense Hydrating Complex (IHC) that penetrates deep into the hair shaft. PM SHINES adds intense hydration and brilliant shine while delivering true-to-tone color. Its gentle formula contains a unique conditioning agent derived from meadowfoam seed that provides exceptional shine and condition with long-lasting, healthy-looking results.

Benefits

- Shine _____

_____

- Hydrating and conditioning _____

_____

- Long lasting _____

_____

Features

- Soy protein _____

_____

- Liquid gel _____

_____

- UV absorber _____

_____

- Clean fragrance _____

_____

How to Measure

- Measure _____

_____

Tips for Mixing PM SHINES

- Measure the Processing Liquid into the beaker or applicator bottle.
- Add the PM SHINES color to the beaker or applicator bottle.
- If using a bowl-and-brush application, pour the contents of the beaker into the mixing bowl. Use a brush or whisk to mix the color into a gel-like consistency.
- If using an applicator-bottle application, place the lid on the bottle, slightly squeeze the bottle, cover the tip of the bottle with your finger, and shake the mixture into a gel-like consistency.

Flash Back™
The 10-Minute Way to Conquer Gray

Turn back time and make male guests look as young as they feel with Flash Back from Paul Mitchell professional hair color. Designed especially for men, Flash Back discreetly conceals gray and white hair in just 10 minutes. Stock your Color Bar with a full range of demi-permanent cool, neutral, and subtly warm tones that deliver the natural-looking, lived-in results men want.

- **Conquers gray hair** — A full range of tones for men, designed to discreetly conceal gray and white hair

- **Natural-looking finish** — Achieves lived-in results with a subtle sheen, allowing men to take years off their look while maintaining a natural appearance

- **10-minute processing time** — Processes quickly to accommodate male guests' need for speed and helps you pick up the pace in the salon

Tips for Mixing Flash Back

Always mix Flash Back with 10-volume Cream or Clear Developer in equal parts (1:1). For example, measure 1 oz or 30 ml of Flash Back + 1 oz or 30 ml 10-volume Cream or Clear Developer.

- Measure 10-volume Cream or Clear Developer into the beaker or applicator bottle.
- Open the bottle and add Flash Back into the beaker or applicator bottle.
- If using a bowl-and-brush application, pour the contents of the beaker into the mixing bowl. Use a brush or mixing whisk to mix the color into a gel-like consistency.
- If using an applicator-bottle application, place the lid on the bottle. Slightly squeeze the bottle, cover the tip of the bottle with your finger, and shake the mixture into a gel-like consistency.
- Process for 10 minutes at room temperature.

Color Shots®

Color Shots are vibrant, pure colors that work seamlessly with both Paul Mitchell **the color** and PM SHINES to give you a whole new world of formulating options. An innovative and multifunctional professional color product, Color Shots can be used to intensify or neutralize semi-, demi-, and permanent color formulations.

The liquid gel consistency mixes easily with Paul Mitchell **the color** and PM SHINES and is completely biodegradable. Each Color Shots bottle comes with a precise dropper that makes measuring a thing of the past.

Benefits

- Pure, vibrant color _____

- Intermixable _____

- Long lasting _____

Features

- Liquid gel _____

- Fresh fragrance _____

- No brown base _____

- List the five Color Shots colors:
  1. _____
  2. _____
  3. _____
  4. _____
  5. _____

How to Measure and Mix

- Recommended amount of Color Shots per 2 oz of color is _____

- Maximum amount of Color Shots per 2 oz of color is _____

Tips for Mixing Color Shots

- Color Shots can be added to Paul Mitchell **the color**, PM SHINES, and Flash Finish.
- Unscrew the dropper from the bottle. Squeeze the dropper to fill the tube to equal one shot.
- Squeeze the dropper to release the product into a mixing bowl or applicator bottle.
- Mix well with a whisk.

Additional Tip

- For even more vibrant reds when using Color Shots red, process an additional 10 minutes.

INKWORKS®

Spark your creativity and add a punch of brilliant color to any canvas with INKWORKS, a gentle formula of pure vibrant pigments in a vegetable base. (View Diagonal Slice — Curly on Disc One.)

Benefits and Features

- 11 brilliant _____

  _____

- Pure vibrant _____

  _____

- Gentle formula _____

  _____

- Ink hair _____

  _____

Tips for Mixing INKWORKS

- Choose the appropriate color or colors.
- Puncture the lid with a T-pin.
- Squeeze the bottle to dispense the product into a mixing bowl.
- If using more than one color, use a mixing brush to mix the colors together inside the mixing bowl.
- For a more pastel or less vibrant result, mix INKWORKS with Super-Charged Moisturizer®.

Color Removers

When faced with lifting already pigmented hair lighter, one of your options is to use a color remover. Color removers shrink artificial pigment and allow room for a new color application and one to two levels of visible change in the hair.

Always follow the manufacturer's instructions when using a color remover. Color removers often include several steps and can differ depending on the brand. If not used properly, the color remover may not shrink enough pigment and could re-darken hair as soon as a new color is added.

Backtrack®
Hair Color Removal System

How often do you get a second chance in life? Give color guests a clean slate and undo past hair color regrets with the Backtrack color removal system. Backtrack contains a mild formula designed to safely lift and remove demi-permanent and permanent hair color without lifting the natural color.

Mild formula — Designed to safely and effectively remove both demi-permanent and permanent hair color without lifting the natural color

Corrective color — Ideal for use directly prior to corrective color applications even on highly processed hair

Custom control — Allows you to process until the desired level of color removal for accurate color correction

Color Block®

Keep color where you want it with Color Block. That beautiful color looks great on hair, but not on the skin.

Protection — This thick, rich cream forms a barrier between the hair color and the skin to help prevent staining

Condition — Emollient, moisturizing conditioners and panthenol treat the hair as it protects

Professional — Excellent for dimensional and Block Color techniques; prevents penetration and deposit of color on the selected sections and helps hold foils in place

Wipe Out®
Prevents and Removes Color Stains

Looking for the ultimate fix for hair color slips? Wipe away hair color stains before they even happen with Wipe Out, an ideal stain barrier and color remover.

Prevents stains — Protects the hairline from staining during the color process

Removes stains — Effectively removes stains and excess color from the hairline and scalp following a color service

Mild formula — Designed to safely and effectively prevent and remove hair color stains without irritation

2 Ways to Color Hair

When understanding the application of hair color, we need to remember that there are only two ways to color the hair: coloring or lightening and foil work. Foil work is divided into weaving and slicing. This concept is the foundation of technique. All coloring techniques expand from this foundation. Let's look at and compare the different ways we color hair.

 Watch and listen to "2 Ways to Color Hair" on Disc One to fill in the blank 2 Ways to Color Hair Chart and to fill in the placement and effect sections in the Color Placement Chart.

2 Ways to Color Hair Chart

ALL-OVER COLOR	FOIL WORK	
COLORING/LIGHTENING	WEAVING	SLICING
Definition:	Definition:	Definition:
Effect:	Effect:	Effect:
When to Use:	When to Use:	When to Use:
Sections:	Sections:	Sections:
Percent of Hair Colored:	Percent of Hair Colored:	Percent of Hair Colored:
Benefit:	Benefit:	Benefit:

Shapes, Placement, and Effect

1. To create dimensional color means to understand…
   a. Shade selection, shapes, and placement.
   b. Color formulation, special effects, and technique.
   c. Height, width, and depth.
   d. Squares, circles, and triangles.

2. When we talk about shapes, we are actually talking about geometry and where you will see…
   a. How a square, circular, or triangular shape falls.
   b. Where shape and geometry live on the hair.
   c. The color living on the hair.
   d. Horizontal, vertical, and diagonal placements.

- Fill in the blank placement boxes by reading the vertical, diagonal, and horizontal techniques in Chapter 5 and The Color System skill cards.

- Fill in the blank effect boxes with the answers to the following questions.
   1. What effect does a horizontal line of color create?
   2. What effect does a diagonal line of color create?
   3. What effect does a vertical line of color create?
   4. How will a horizontal line of color fall?
   5. How will a diagonal line of color fall?
   6. How will a vertical line of color fall?
   7. To what point do the ends fall on a horizontal line?
   8. To what point do the ends fall on a diagonal line?
   9. To what point do the ends fall on a vertical line?

Activity

Practice on a doll head to see which effects you can create by coloring squares, triangles, and circles.

- Which effects do you achieve with one-length, graduated, and layered haircuts?
- Which effects do you achieve with short, medium, or longer lengths?
- Which effects do you achieve with straight, wavy, curly, or extra curly hair?

The combinations are endless. Be creative and have fun!

Color Placement Chart

CUTTING TECHNIQUE	EFFECT	PLACEMENT	EFFECT	KEY POINTS	EXAMPLES
One-Length	0° elevation Maximum density Minimum movement			Place the color on the top of the head for maximum results.	
Graduation	1-89° elevation Buildup of weight Side-to-side movement			Place the color on the top and sides of the head. *Avoid working the color below the line of graduation.	
Layers	90°+ elevation Removal of weight Maximum movement			Place the color throughout the head. *Except on short layers.	

Dimensional Color or Block Color

The combination of foil work and tinting gives us dimensional coloring or Block Color.

This technique provides options that are more interesting for the guest. It allows for less time and more money when customizing. It also personalizes your color-making ability, making you indispensable to your guest. Dimensional or Block Color also allows you to maximize your cut — it can be a whisper, a talk, or a shout, depending on the placement and colors used.

Activity

Find pictures that represent "Whisper, Talk, and Shout" hair color and glue them into a binder to create your own personal "look book." Make it colorful and creative.

Learning Review

Read

In color theory, identify what you will focus on to improve your understanding.

Reflect

What did you learn about the two ways to color hair? How will you use this information in your guest services?

Review

View the DVD, Disc Two, Color Theory. Use the Interactive Color Map to test your knowledge by completing the activity in Chapter 6.

Select/Prioritize

Review and identify the steps to formulation. Practice formulation using the formulation worksheet.

Draw

Create a windowpane for the steps for measuring and mixing each of the Paul Mitchell color and lightening products.

Share/Act

Teach what you have learned to a friend or coworker.

The Color System

PAUL MITCHELL schools

Chapter 3
Guest Experience

Staging the Color Experience

Extraordinary Service

Greeting

Consultation

Service

Completion

Guest Experience

Assuring the comfort and satisfaction of your guest is vital to a great service experience. A thorough consultation and the proper service area setup are the first steps to building your guest's confidence and loyalty. A comfortable guest is a happy guest and happy guests return and refer their friends. In this chapter, you will learn the steps to staging an extraordinary color service, proper service area setup, and thorough color consultations.

 ## Words to Remember

Before you begin, learn the key terms in this chapter. Locate the terms in the glossary.

Dominant pigment	Lift	Porosity
Highlift hair color	Lowlight	
Level	Natural level	

12 Gotta Dos of Hair Color Services

1. Be informed. Know your products, tools, and application techniques for achieving the desired color results.

2. Determine the natural level of the hair (at the scalp), the canvas level of the hair (after the line of demarcation), and the desired result of the service.

3. Perform a hair analysis including:
   - Elasticity
   - Porosity
   - Texture

4. Check for lighting, tone, and depth. Use this information when formulating.

5. Determine the percentage of gray (look at the natural hair by the scalp).

6. Discuss the guest's previous chemical services (including color and texture services).

7. Discuss a pretreatment plan to achieve the desired results.

8. Perform a patch test on the guest.

9. Discuss the plan of action for achieving the desired results with the guest based on this information.

10. Discuss the post-color treatment and recommend the proper products for maintaining the desired results.

11. Book the guest's next appointment to maintain the color service.

12. Make this and every service an extraordinary one for you and your guest!

 Activity

Create a learning map or windowpane of the 12 Gotta Dos of Hair Color Services.

Staging the Color Experience

Sanitary Maintenance Area (SMA) and Setup

The area in which you set up, organize, and maintain cleanliness is known as a **sanitary maintenance area** or **SMA**. All tools including gloves, clips, combs, foils, color brush, bowl, and towel are neatly placed on a paper towel. Presentation is everything! See Figure 3-1.

You will feel more confident, organized, and prepared for your service guest with the proper setup. The guest will feel comfortable and confident in your service when you present yourself professionally.

Figure 3-1

Draping

Draping will protect the guest's skin and clothing from water, color, lightener, perms, chemical relaxer, etc. It is important to keep a clean and sanitary surface next to the guest's skin.

Preparation for Draping the Guest

1. Gather the proper materials and supplies.

2. Sanitize your hands.

3. Seat the service guest comfortably and ask the guest to remove all neck and hair jewelry. Give it to the guest to store safely.

4. Remove any remaining objects from the guest's hair.

5. Smoothly turn the guest's collar to the inside of his or her shirt, if applicable.

6. Proceed to drape for the applicable service.

Draping for Wet Hair Services

Single Drape Procedure

1. Complete the preparation steps for draping.
2. Place the towel lengthwise across the service guest's shoulders, so that one-third of the width is upward around the neck with the remainder draped across the head.
3. Overlap the ends of the towel under the chin.
4. Position the cape around the portion of the towel around the guest's neck.
5. Fasten and secure the cape in the back.
6. Fold the top one-third of the towel down around the cape.

Draping for Chemical Services

Double Drape Procedure

1. Complete the preparation steps for draping.
2. Place the towel lengthwise across the service guest's shoulders, so that one-third of the width is upward around the neck with the remainder draped across the shoulders.
3. Overlap the ends of the towel under the chin.
4. Drape a second towel, so that one-third of the width is down around the neck with the remainder draped across the top of the head.
5. Position the cape around the portion of the towels around the guest's neck.
6. Fasten and secure the cape in the back.
7. Fold the top two-thirds of the towel down around the cape.

   On which live model is a double drape demonstrated? _____

Activity
Place "SD" for single drape and "DD" for double drape next to the service.

Double process	_____	Upstyle	_____
Haircut	_____	Chemical relaxer	_____
Block Color	_____	Color weave	_____
Single process	_____	Style and finish	_____
Shampoo and style	_____	Men's haircut	_____
Color slice	_____	Permanent wave	_____

Extraordinary Service

Extraordinary service is the result of extraordinary performances from the service desk team, Learning Leaders, and future and salon professionals. The service experience has four action steps, including the greeting, consultation, service, and completion. Within each aspect of the service, many opportunities exist to service guests, solve their challenges, and sell more services and Take Home products. Let's explore how to connect with guests and positively influence the decisions they make about their image.

The 10 Opportunities outline the service opportunities to build guest retention, rebookings, and increase Take Home and additional service sales.

10 Opportunities

There are opportunities to connect with and serve your guests in each part of the service.

1. *Create Magic First!* — Always greet your guests with a "Be Nice" welcome. Use their first and last name, be friendly, and escort them to your service area.

2. *Identify Challenges* — Discover what your guests need and look for opportunities to serve them by asking discovery questions.

3. *Recommend Solutions* — Suggest services and products to help your guests. Get their agreement before you proceed with the service.

4. *The Wash House* — Create a customized product experience. Allow your guests to choose a Wash House experience from the menu.

5. *Educate Your Guests* — Provide information that will help your guests look and feel better by taking time to share ideas and tips about their beauty and image throughout the entire service.

6. *Talk Professionally* — Focus on your guests and direct your conversations to their needs. Be present and with your guests at all times.

7. *The Color Bar* — Create a color experience or another service your guests may need to enhance their image.

8. *Style Experience* — Show your guests which products to use and how to create and maintain their new look.

9. *Review Recommendations* — Review what you recommend, write down your recommendations, and answer questions at your service area.

10. *2-Minute Plan* — Follow the steps of the 2-Minute Plan.

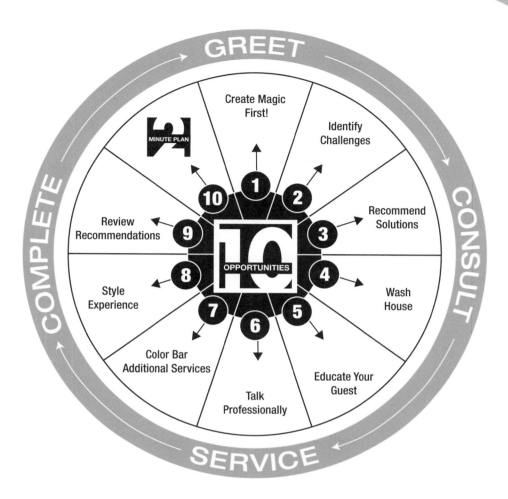

Activity

Take a moment to review the old script/new script. Identify three scripts that you must work on and focus on in your consultations. Once you have mastered three scripts, choose another three to incorporate and continue until you are consistently using the new scripts. Share your scripts with a learning partner.

Old Script	*New Script*
Client	Guest
Student	Future professional
Stylist	Salon professional
Hi, hey, hello…	Good morning/afternoon/evening
Hi.	Welcome
Can I help you?	How may I assist you?
Book an appointment	Reserve time
Running late	A bit behind schedule
You're welcome; no problem	My pleasure
Okay; sure thing!	Certainly
Mistake	Discovery
Sorry about that…	Please forgive me; I apologize

Greeting

One of the most important skills you can perform is to professionally greet your guests. Future and salon professionals must practice greetings. Have a partner provide feedback and coaching to build excellent service habits. Work with others to enhance your verbal and nonverbal communication skills including your:

- **Smile and eye contact**
- **Posture and body proximity**
- **Handshake**
- **Tone of voice and greeting dialogue**

Here are the four basic steps to a professional greeting:

STEP 1: **Professionally acknowledge the guest.**

When you enter the Take Home or seating area, you will want to identify your guest. Walk up to the guest and say, *"Hello, are you _____ (say the guest's first and last name)?"*

Avoid announcing names loudly across the entire area. This may be embarrassing to some guests and it lacks professionalism.

STEP 2: **Warmly welcome the guest.**

You may say, *"Hi. Welcome. My name is _____. I am so happy to meet you..."* or *"Welcome, _____ (guest's name). It is great to see you again."*

A warm welcome includes a smile, eye contact, and confident handshake.

STEP 3: **Describe and direct the guest.**

Put guests at ease by providing a clear description of what they may expect. Say, *"Please walk with me back to my service area. My service area is _____ (describe where it is)."* Then direct the way.

STEP 4: **Escort the guest.**

You must walk side by side with your guests, showing them the way.

Consultation

The goal of the guest consultation is to identify your guests' vision for their skin, makeup, or hair and to create a game plan of how to create a look that they will love. It is your role as the skilled and knowledgeable future and salon professional to guide your guests through the decision-making process. Guests won't always know what they want or need. They need you to help them to figure that out.

During the consultation, you also have the opportunity to gain a guest's trust and to help him or her relax.

The best way to get your guests to trust and like you is to show that you are interested in helping them. You can learn about your guests, build their trust, and connect with them by:

- **Asking a lot of questions to uncover their vision of their image.**
- **Listening to what they say and observing their body language.**

If you are focused and taking time with the consultation, you will uncover important clues and information that will lead to your guest's satisfaction in the final outcome.

Connect by asking questions. There is an art to questioning. Open-ended questions usually bring better, more detailed responses. Ask open-ended questions to gather information about what the guest likes and dislikes. Confirm with closed questions before you move forward.

Activity

A few examples of open-ended questions are:
How much time and money do you usually spend on your hair?
What does your current hair regimen look like?

Closed-ended questions include:
Do you like the red tones?
Do you want to avoid going lighter?

Forward-focused questions include:
What do you like best about your hair?
What would you like to experience during your service today?

Create your own list of questions that you will use in your guest consultations.

Prior to beginning the consultation, ensure the guest is at eye level and you are facing him or her.

◼ **Guest Service Form —** The guest completes the personal information on the guest profile card or consultation card.

◼ **Needs Analysis —** Ask a variety of questions to determine the guest's needs and desires, such as:

- "What do you like about your hair color?"
- "When was the last time you colored your hair?"
- "What are your expectations for your hair color today?"
- "What is your budget for your hair color service?"

◼ **Experience Menu —** Place the experience menu in the guest's hands.

◼ **Make a Recommendation —** Make and confirm a service and Take Home recommendation, including a shampoo and conditioner, saying, "Based on what you have told me, I recommend ..."

You may tell the guest:

"I would like to introduce our Color Bar menu today. On it, you will find _____, which would be a great service with our allotted time today. It will enhance your shine and build back protein."

◼ **Take Home Recommendation Form —** Write the Take Home product recommendation on the Take Home recommendation form.

◼ **The Wash House —** Show the guest The Wash House menu and describe the Wash House service you will perform.

 Activity

With a learning partner, role-play and practice a color consultation using the following:

- Guest service form
- Forward-focused, open-ended questions
- The Wash House menu
- The Color Bar menu
- Take Home menu
- Take Home recommendation form

Provide each other with feedback on what you did well and what you could improve.

Watch and listen to the live consultations for the model on Disc One to answer the questions.

Single Process — Tracy

1. List all of the colorful or descriptive words that Linda and Kate say during Tracy's consultation.

   _____

   _____

2. Which technique is used on Tracy?

   _____

   _____

3. Which product is used?

   _____

   _____

4. According to Linda, what benefit or feature will this product give to Tracy's hair?

   _____

   _____

5. Is porosity an issue? Why?

   _____

   _____

6. What is Tracy's hair fabric rating?

   _____

   _____

7. What contributed to this rating?

   _____

   _____

8. What is the pretreatment formula for Tracy's hair?

   _____

   _____

9. Which color formula is selected?
   Formula 1_____

   _____

Watch and listen to the live consultations for the model on Disc One to answer the questions.

Double Process — Jamie

1. List all of the colorful or descriptive words that Linda and Lucie say during Jamie's consultation.

    _____

    _____

2. Which technique is used on Jamie?

    _____

    _____

3. What concerns are expressed about Jamie's hair?

    _____

    _____

4. Which product is used first? What features or benefits does this product have?
    Formula 1_____

    _____

5. Which product and color are used second? What are the benefits?
    Formula 2_____

    _____

Watch and listen to the live consultations for the model on Disc One to answer the questions.

Vertical Slice: Option A, Horseshoe — Katie

1. List all of the colorful or descriptive words that Linda and Kate say during Katie's consultation.

   _____

   _____

2. Is Katie's hair pre-colored?

   _____

   _____

3. Is Katie's hair naturally curly or straight?

   _____

   _____

4. Which technique is used on Katie?

   _____

   _____

5. Which color formula is selected?
   Formula 1_____

   _____

   Formula 2_____

   _____

6. What is Highlift? Why is it used?

   _____

   _____

7. What are Color Shots?

   _____

   _____

8. Why are Color Shots used in this formulation?

   _____

   _____

Watch and listen to the live consultations for the model on Disc One to answer the questions.

Vertical Slice: Option B, Boxes — Whitney

1. List all of the colorful or descriptive words that Linda and Audra say during Whitney's consultation.

   _____

   _____

2. Which technique is used on Whitney?

   _____

   _____

3. How many rows are used? Why?

   _____

   _____

4. How many color formulas are used? Why?

   _____

   _____

5. Which color formula is selected?
   Formula 1_____

   _____

   Formula 2_____

   _____

   Formula 3_____

   _____

Watch and listen to the live consultations for the model on Disc One to answer the questions.

Diagonal Slice: Straight Hair — Jessica

1. List all of the colorful or descriptive words that Linda and Audra say during Jessica's consultation.

   _____

   _____

2. Does color lift or lighten artificial color?

   _____

   _____

3. Which type of haircut does Jessica have?

   _____

   _____

4. Which technique is used on Jessica?

   _____

   _____

5. What is Jessica's natural level?

   _____

   _____

6. Which color formula is selected? How are the formulas applied?

   Formula 1_____

   _____

   Formula 2_____

   _____

   Formula 3_____

   _____

Watch and listen to the live consultations for the model on Disc One to answer the questions.

Diagonal Slice: Curly Hair — Melinda

1. List all of the colorful or descriptive words that Linda and Kate say during Melinda's consultation.

   _____

   _____

2. What shape is Melinda's hair cut in?

   _____

3. Did Melinda have her hair colored in a salon or did she color it at home?

   _____

4. Which technique is used on Melinda? What variation does Kate make based on Melinda's hair?

   _____

   _____

5. What is done on Melinda to achieve a bolder result?

   _____

6. Before coloring Melinda's hair, what pretreatment is used? Why?

   _____

   _____

7. What story does Kate want to tell? Which product does she use to tell the story?

   _____

   _____

8. What are Formulas 1 and 2? How are the formulas applied?
   Formula 1_____

   _____

   Formula 2_____

   _____

9. What does Kate say about INKWORKS?

   _____

10. Does Kate know what colors she will use to tell the story? Why?

    _____

    _____

Watch and listen to the live consultations for the model on Disc One to answer the questions.

Horizontal Weave — Desiree

1. List all of the colorful or descriptive words that Linda and Audra say during Desiree's consultation.

   _____

   _____

2. What is Desiree's natural level?

   _____

3. What is Desiree's mid-shaft level?

   _____

4. Which technique is used on Desiree?

   _____

5. What defines a lowlight?

   _____

   _____

6. What is the function of outside automatic formulation?

   _____

   _____

7. How many levels of lift are desired?

   _____

8. What is Desiree's dominant pigment? How is the dominant pigment controlled?

   _____

9. What are the four formulas? How are the formulas applied?

   _____

   _____

10. Two things need to happen to achieve a more natural blending of colors for Desiree. What are they?

   _____

   _____

Service

The goal of every service is to create an experience. Consider the services you provide from your guest's perspective.

Become guest-focused

Put yourself in your guest's shoes and ask, *"What would I like to experience?"* Each of your guests is unique. Your goal is to provide your guests with an experience that meets their specific expectations, preferences, and needs.

Think of the service in terms of what the guest will experience rather than what you will do. This will help you develop sensitivity to your guest's unique needs and, in turn, build a long-term relationship with him or her.

Offer pleasant surprises

Surprise your guest with an extra long head massage during the shampoo, a hand massage using Lavender Mint Moisturizing Body Butter™ or Lemon Sage Energizing Body Lotion™ during a chemical service, or a gourmet drink in a spotless glass. Great service experiences are filled with pleasant surprises that help guests enjoy and relax while they allow you to work your magic. Those added touches make your guests feel that they are on center stage. Pamper, listen, recommend, and solve your guests' challenges. The more you can solve their challenges, the more connected and loyal your guests will become.

Brand your professional service

You will want to practice providing professional service and Take Home recommendations. Use the Take Home recommendation form and your business card to make service and future reservations, as well as Take Home product recommendations.

Activity

Create a list of "pleasant surprises" you could offer your guests during their color service.

Completion

The completion process at the end of the service is especially important for ensuring that your guests' needs and expectations have been met. Complete these steps:

- Educate your guests on how to maintain their look. Say, *"Today, I used* (product name)." Explain the product benefits.

- Complete and review a Take Home recommendation form and hand it to the guest.

- Say, "(Guest's name), *here are the products I recommend to take home to maintain what we have created today."* Review all recommendations. Ask, *"What questions do you have about your hair color?"*

- Complete the service ticket with additional product charges.

- Complete the Take Home recommendation form and/or business card with the recommendation of a future reservation date and/or additional services. Say, *"You should also return in five weeks to maintain your color, which is* (state the date). *How does that work for you?"*

Rebooking Tip:

When recommending that guests return, give them a specific date, saying, *"To maintain your look, I recommend you return for* (say service) *on or about* (state the date)." Be sure to write the date on the back of the business card.

Activity

Practice your rebooking dialogue with a learning partner.

Completion Checklist ✓

Completion at the Service Area

■ **Confirm and Review Take Home** — Complete all service forms and the Take Home recommendation form and review all service and Take Home product recommendations with the guest.

■ **Ask for a Referral** — At the service area, tell your guests that you loved working with them and would love to work with their friends and family. Give your guests a few extra business cards and invite them to share the cards with their friends and family.

■ **Future Reservation** — Share when the guests must return for the next service to maintain their look. Write the exact recommended date on the Take Home recommendation form or on the back of a business card.

■ **2-Minute Plan**

Complete the guest's experience by following our service completion process.

1. Wait to clean your service area.

2. Escort your guest to the service desk.

3. Introduce your guest to the service team.

4. Pull products, focus on solutions, and make recommendations.

5. Reserve a future service time.

6. Give your guest a business card and five more business cards.

7. Ask for a referral.

8. Say thank you.

9. Clean your service area.

 ## Activity

To memorize the 2-Minute Plan, create a song, rap, poem, or skit about the 2-Minute Plan. Share it with your learning partner.

Guest Follow-up

What can you do to connect with your guests between services? Two great ways include follow-up calls and thank-you notes.

Follow-Up Call

Ensure your guests are enjoying their new look by calling them following the service.

Your follow-up call script:

Ask: *"Hi,* (guest name). *It's* (your name) *from* (school or salon name).

Do you have a moment?" If you have caught the guest at a bad time, offer to call back at a better time. Ask what time would be convenient.

Say: *"I just wanted to follow up to make sure that your hair color is working well for you."* Wait for your guest to describe how he or she is feeling about the service. It is important that your guest knows that you are listening and interested.

Ask: *"Are you able to style your hair the way you wanted?"* or *"How does your color look after you style your hair?"* Let your guest answer. Respond to your guest in a calm and relaxed manner.

You may also ask about the guest's product purchase. *"How are you enjoying your products?"* and *"Do you have any questions about how to use them?"*

Thank your guests when you receive a positive response. You may also confirm the next reservation or recommend scheduling another reservation.

Say: *"I am happy that you are enjoying your products and hair color. We'll see you* (date/time)." (Or) *"I hope to see you soon. Thank you for taking the time to speak with me."*

Activity

With a learning partner, practice and role-play a guest follow-up call. Provide each other with feedback on what you did well and what you could improve.

Guest Follow-up

continued

Responding to Follow-Up Calls

If your guest's response is not so positive, remember to listen and stay focused on solutions. View a guest's feedback as an opportunity to gain his or her loyalty by offering excellent follow-up service. The following are some suggestions to respond to your guest's challenges:

- Ask questions about the guest's challenge.

- Listen patiently until you have resolved the challenge.

- Provide suggestions on how to correct the challenge. In extreme cases, offer to have your guests return so you may look at their hair.

- Remain relaxed and calm. Your guests may not return if they think you are upset or angry.

- Say, *"I am happy we were able to create a follow-up plan,* (guest's name). *I just want you to know that I appreciate your business and want you to be completely satisfied with your look and your products. I will see you on* (date/time). *Thank you."*

Send a Thank-You Note

Another great way to have your guest fondly remember you is to send a thank-you note within two days of the service. Take a moment to thank your guests for their business and invite them back. You may want to enclose your business card with a reminder date and time of the scheduled reservation.

If you really want to connect with your loyal guests, remember their birthdays and send birthday cards. This is a wonderful little surprise that will remind them of you and the unbelievable service and support you provide them.

Thank You!

Dear Veronica,

Thank you for a great visit. I am happy that you love your hair color and appreciate your business. Hope to see you again. If you have any questions, call me at [list telephone number].

Thank you.

Janet

 Color Experience Checklist ✓

Greet — Connect with your guest.

■ Obtain the guest service ticket and chemical service record. Learn your guest's name and the color service requested.

■ Welcome your guest with a smile and use a professional greeting as outlined.

■ Give all new guests a tour of the clinic floor or salon; describe Take Home, The Tool Bar, The Wash House, and The Color Bar. Introduce The Color Bar as our center for creating an extraordinary color experience. Share that we love to celebrate hair color here!

■ Escort your guest to your service area (station), which is completely preset to offer an extraordinary color service experience.

■ Assist your guest into the chair and place the experience menu into his or her hands.

■ Put your guest at ease by sharing a compliment with him or her.

Consult — Uncover your guest's needs and create a color formulation.

■ Drape your guest using the appropriate draping technique.

■ Ask open-ended questions to guide your guest through the consultation and document his or her responses on a guest profile information card.

■ Use the experience menu in the consultation.

■ Make recommendations by saying, "Here is what I recommend we do today," then describe the service and color technique.

■ Recommend a service upgrade and say, "What do you think about our plan?" Confirm your guest's requests.

■ Recommend a Take Home category on the experience menu.

■ Confirm all formulations and techniques before beginning all color services.

■ Go to The Color Bar to obtain your color tools and products.

■ While mixing the color, share with your guests the benefits of using professional hair color and what results they may expect.

Service — Create a color experience.

■ Apply the color using the appropriate techniques.

■ Be sure that your service and work areas are clean. Use the clean-as-you-go method. As soon as you spill or drip color, wipe it up! Check the guest's hairline, ears, and neck and remove any excess color.

■ Describe to your guest what the processing time should be. During the processing time, offer a hand massage with Lavender Mint Moisturizing Body Butter™ or Lemon Sage Energizing Body Lotion™.

■ Offer a service upgrade, which may include a haircut, manicure service, or makeup application to be conducted after the color service.

■ Select the styling products you will use and recommend and write them on the Take Home recommendation form.

Color Experience Checklist ✓

continued

- Teach your guests how to maintain their hair color. Describe the shampoo and conditioner they will need to use for their color upkeep, take the products to the service area, and put them in their hands so they can see and smell them.

- Record the formulations and processing instructions on the chemical record card.

- Check the processing of the color before rinsing.

- Use the appropriate techniques for rinsing and shampooing at The Wash House. Review the proper rinsing and shampooing techniques on the DVD. Clean the sink after rinsing and shampooing your guest.

- Conduct the style consultation and confirm the styling techniques. Use the appropriate styling products and follow the proper styling techniques and procedures.

- Educate your guest about the tools and products you use to create the finished style. Teach him or her how to use the styling product (i.e., how much to apply).

- After completing the style, share styling tips so your guest can re-create the same look at home.

Complete — Summarize your guest's experience and conduct the 2-Minute Plan.

At your service area:

- *Review the Take Home recommendations* — Say, "To maintain your look, I recommend you take these products home with you today."

- *Rebook your guests* — Say, "In addition, you are going to notice that you will need to have your hair color freshened in about four to five weeks, which is (state an exact date). Let's see if we can reschedule you for then."

- *Ask for a referral* — You may also say, "What do you think of your hair?" and if your guest likes it, you may say, "I'm very happy you like it. I enjoyed working with you today and would love to work with your family and friends; may I give you a few extra cards for them?"

- Remove the cape and assist your guest out of the styling chair.

2-Minute Plan:

- Carry the Take Home products and Take Home recommendation form to the service desk.

- Introduce the Service Desk Coordinator and ask him or her to check the schedule for future reservations.

- If you do not have the Take Home products, pull them while the Service Desk Coordinator completes your guest's reservation and purchase.

- If you did not ask for a referral at your service area, hand your guest five business cards and say, "Here are a few extra business cards. If you liked what I did today, I would be grateful for any referrals — I promise I will take great care of your family and friends."

- Thank your guest for coming in!

- Clean your service area. Celebrate your great work!

Activity: Color Consultation and Take Home

1. Number the steps of the 10 Opportunities in the proper order.
   _____ The Wash House
   _____ Review Recommendations
   _____ Talk Professionally
   _____ Identify Challenges
   _____ Educate Your Guests
   _____ The Color Bar
   _____ Create Magic First!
   _____ Style Experience
   _____ 2-Minute Plan
   _____ Recommend Solutions

2. Fill out three guest profile cards using three other learners acting as your service guests.
   _____
   _____
   _____

3. Fill out three chemical service record cards using three other learners acting as your service guests.
   _____
   _____
   _____

4. Write three forward-focused questions for a hair color consultation.
   _____
   _____
   _____

5. Draw a line to match the old terminology to the new terminology:

Old Color Words	New Color Words
Roots	Lightener
Hydrogen peroxide	Highlight
Dye	Color
Frost	Developer
Bleach	**the color** Map
Color wheel	New growth

6. You can create an extraordinary guest experience by paying attention to details and engaging the guest's five senses. How will you engage the guest's senses when performing a color service?

   1. Visual _____

   2. Smell _____

   3. Taste _____

   4. Hearing _____

   5. Touch _____

7. List all of the Take Home products that are designed for color-treated hair.

   _____

   _____

   _____

8. Using the Take Home menu, determine which products you would recommend for:

   Colored hair _____

   _____

   _____

   Double-process blonde _____

   _____

   _____

   Colored and permed hair _____

   _____

   _____

   Colored and relaxed hair _____

   _____

   _____

   Highlighted hair _____

   _____

   _____

9. Write three forward-focused questions for a color service follow-up telephone call.

   _____

   _____

   _____

Learning Review

Read

In this chapter, identify what you will focus on to improve the guest experience.

Reflect

What did you learn about extraordinary service? How will you use it?

Review

Create your own extraordinary service checklist. Be sure to include the greeting, consultation, service, and completion.

Select/Prioritize

Identify pleasant surprises that you will implement in your guest services.

Draw

Create a windowpane for the steps of the 10 Opportunities and 2-Minute Plan.

Share/Act

Teach what you have learned to a friend or coworker.

The Color System

PAUL MITCHELL schools

Chapter 4
Lightening, Coloring, and Diagramming

Diagramming

Single-Process Color

Double-Process Color

Platinum Card

Rinsing and Shampooing

Lightening, Coloring, and Diagramming

Your confidence as a hair colorist will soar as you master the application techniques to achieve beautiful all-over color. This chapter will assist you in learning the step-by-step sectioning and application techniques for all-over color services: a new approach to single- and double-process color and Platinum Card. You will also discover the proper rinsing and shampooing process necessary to complete a successful color service.

 Words to Remember

Before you begin, learn the key terms in this chapter. Locate the terms in the glossary.

Apex	Line of demarcation	Panel
Bleeding	Mastoid division line	Section
Emulsify	Mastoid process	Segment
Holiday	Nape	Slice or slicing
Hot spot	Occipital	Weave or weaving

Diagramming

Diagram 1

Single or Double Process

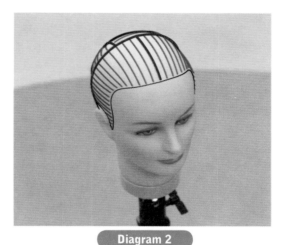

Diagram 2

Horizontal Weave

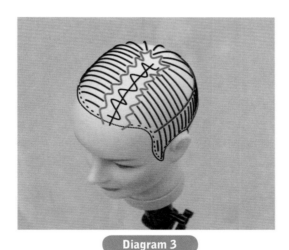

Diagram 3

Vertical Slice, Horseshoe

When learning a haircut, color technique, style, or finish method, diagramming is an essential skill and the most effective way of note taking. Diagramming is also a great way to communicate your ideas to other hairstylists.

To improve your diagramming skills, first you need to know the definitions of segment, panel, and section and then follow these diagramming tips.

- **Segment —** The hair can be divided into four to five segments. More than five segments are known as *panels.*

- **Panel —** A smaller area within a segment is called a *panel.*

- **Section —** A smaller, workable area within a panel or segment, when coloring or cutting, is generally ¼ of an inch or less in size. The hair that is to be sliced or weaved is known as a *section.*

Diagramming Tips

1. When diagramming, always use colored pencils or pens. Contrasting colors such as blue, green, and red make the division between segments, panels, and sections easier to see.
2. To clearly distinguish between segments, panels, and sections, choose at least three colors.
3. You can create two diagrams: one diagram for the sections of the technique and the other diagram for the color application.
4. Write the name of the technique, color formula, processing times, and any notes on the diagram.
5. Include all information, such as where to begin the sectioning, where to begin the application, and any technique key points to ensure that you can interpret your diagrams.
6. Use numbers on the diagrams to correspond with the steps of any written instructions. Keep in mind that the order of sectioning may be different from the order of application.
7. Presentation is everything! Always use rulers and protractors to diagram.
8. For better organization, use multiple head sheets when diagramming shapes that contain multiple steps and additional information.
9. When drawing the diagram, it may be easier to draw the sections in the same order that you would section the hair.
10. When diagramming, remember you are compressing a three-dimensional object into two dimensions and it may require a lot of practice to become successful at it.

Color Diagramming Key

• ||||	**Use multiple colors**
• ••••••••••	**Hairline**
• - - - - - - -	**To drop out or section out the hairline**
• ⌇⌇⌇⌇⌇	**Natural part**
• wwwwww	**Zigzag parting**
• ▬▬▬▬	**Segments or panels**
• ———	**Sections**

Single-Process Color

A single-process color lightens and/or deposits in a single application. Examples of single-process coloring are virgin application, retouch applications, and gray coverage applications. Single-process color can be applied using a bottle or a bowl and brush. Always wear gloves when applying hair color.

before

after

Technique Key Points

Watch and listen to "Technique Key Points — Single Process" on Disc One to fill in the blanks.

1. Create your _____ _____.

2. Start your application in the _____.

3. Work from _____ to _____.

4. Take _____ sections in the back and _____ sections at the sides.

5. Make sure _____ is consistent.

6. Make sure there is no _____ around the _____ or _____.

7. Make sure there are no _____.

What key points would you add to this list?

_____

_____

Service Area Setup

Watch and listen to the sanitary maintenance area (SMA) setup in "SMA & Setup" on Disc One to list the basic tools required to begin this technique.

Tools and Equipment

- ☐ _____
- ☐ _____
- ☐ _____
- ☐ _____
- ☐ _____
- ☐ _____
- ☐ _____
- ☐ _____
- ☐ _____
- ☐ _____
- ☐ _____

What else do you need to add to this list to stage an extraordinary service experience?

- ☐ _____
- ☐ _____
- ☐ _____
- ☐ _____
- ☐ _____
- ☐ _____
- ☐ _____
- ☐ _____
- ☐ _____

Review the DVD and skill card for product and tool options.

Diagramming

Watch and listen to the technique key points for this technique on Disc One. Make note of any additional diagramming tips.

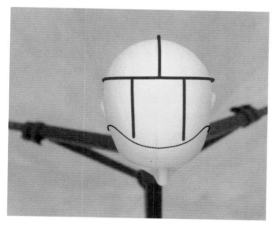

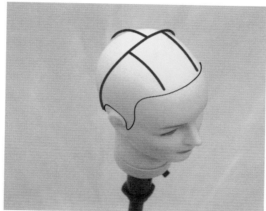

Activity

On a separate head sheet, practice diagramming this technique.

Parting the Hair for a Single Process

Follow these steps for a successful single-process color application.

1. Begin parting a mastoid division line from the apex to the mastoid process on both sides, separating the front from the back.

2. Create a vertical part from the apex to the center nape, separating the back into two segments. Clip both segments.

3. In the front segment, create a Mohawk panel by parting the hair using the center of the eye as a guide. Create a horizontal line from the hairline above the eye to the mastoid division line.

4. You will now have five segments. Clip each segment. See Figure 4-1.

Figure 4-1

Five segments

Applying Hair Color

Figure 4-2

Outline segments

1. Beginning in the back, outline one segment with color. See Figure 4-2.

2. Starting at the bottom of that same panel, take ¼-inch horizontal sections and apply color to each section progressing to the top of the segment.

3. Outline the other back segment. Move to the bottom; taking ¼-inch horizontal sections, apply color to each section progressing to the top of the segment.

4. Move to a side panel and outline with color.

5. Start at the mastoid division line; taking ¼-inch vertical sections, apply color to each section progressing to the front hairline.

Applying Hair Color
continued

6. Lay each vertical section back and away from the face.
7. Repeat Steps 4, 5, and 6 on the other side.
8. Move to the Mohawk segment.
9. Starting at the apex, take ¼-inch sections and apply color to each section, progressing to the front hairline.
10. Lay each colored section back and away from the face.
11. The processing time is based on the manufacturer's recommendations.
12. Rinse with warm water until the water runs clear.
13. Shampoo and condition based on the manufacturer's recommendations.

Note: This single-process technique is not designed to replace recommended state board guidelines for virgin, retouch, and gray coverage color applications.

Notes

Activity
Using a learning map or windowpane, write the steps for the sectioning and application of single-process color.

Quality Check

After processing the color or lightener, shampooing, conditioning, and styling, it is important to check the quality of your work. With a doll head and on a color service guest, take random horizontal sections throughout the hair.

Figure 4-3

- Are the results even from the scalp through the ends? See Figure 4-3.
- Are there any holidays?
- Is the hairline clean? See Figure 4-4.
- Do you have complete saturation?

Figure 4-4

What did you discover? _____
_____
_____
_____
_____
_____

How can you improve next time? _____
_____
_____
_____
_____
_____
_____

Review the skill card for this technique.

⊙ Review

1. Where does the application start and why?

   _____

   _____

2. What size of horizontal sections should you take when applying color?

   _____

3. What types of sections are taken starting at the mastoid division line?

   _____

4. How is the Mohawk panel created?

   _____

   _____

5. What is the purpose of outlining and only working the color in one segment at a time?

   _____

6. Why should you apply color from the bottom of the segment to the top?

   _____

7. How does taking vertical sections in the front segments help you to work cleanly and efficiently?

   _____

   _____

8. Why should you rinse the hair with warm water until it runs clear?

   _____

   _____

9. How do you create the five standard segments and why?

   _____

   _____

   _____

   _____

10. What are you looking for when performing a quality check for single-process color?

   _____

   _____

   _____

   _____

Double-Process Color

A double-process application first decolorizes or lightens the hair and then requires a second application of color to tone the hair into a more desirable color. Always wear gloves when applying lightener and toner.

before

after

Technique Key Points

 Watch and listen to the "Technique Key Points — Double Process" on Disc One. Number the steps in the proper order.

_____ Apply the lightener to the scalp, taking ⅛-inch horizontal sections.

_____ Start your application in the back.

_____ Make sure there are no holidays.

_____ Take horizontal sections in the back and vertical sections at the sides.

_____ Work from bottom to top.

_____ Outline panels, applying lightener to the scalp.

_____ Make sure coverage is consistent.

_____ Create your five panels.

What key points would you add to this list?

_____

_____

Service Area Setup

 Watch and listen to the sanitary maintenance area (SMA) setup in "SMA & Setup" on Disc One to list the basic tools required to begin this technique.

Tools and Equipment

- [ ] _____
- [ ] _____
- [ ] _____
- [ ] _____
- [ ] _____
- [ ] _____
- [ ] _____
- [ ] _____
- [ ] _____
- [ ] _____
- [ ] _____
- [ ] _____

What else do you need to add to this list to stage an extraordinary service experience?

- [ ] _____
- [ ] _____
- [ ] _____
- [ ] _____
- [ ] _____
- [ ] _____
- [ ] _____
- [ ] _____
- [ ] _____

  Review the DVD and skill card for product and tool options.

Diagramming

 Watch and listen to the technique key points for this technique on Disc One. Make note of any additional diagramming tips.

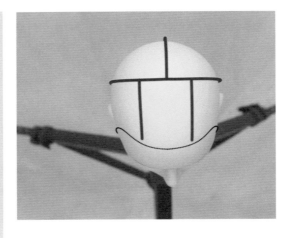

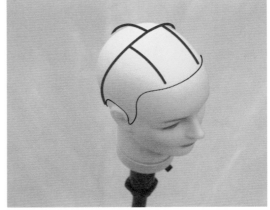

 ## Activity

On a separate head sheet, practice diagramming this technique.

Parting the Hair for a Double Process

Figure 4-5

Five segments

Follow these steps for a successful double-process color application.

1. Begin parting a mastoid division line from the apex to the mastoid process on both sides, separating the front from the back.

2. Create a vertical part from the apex to the center nape, separating the back into two segments. Clip both segments.

3. In the front segment, create a Mohawk panel by parting the hair using the center of the eye as a guide. Create a horizontal line from the hairline above the eye to the mastoid division line.

4. You will now have five segments. Clip each segment. See Figure 4-5.

Applying Lightener

Figure 4-6

Applying lightener

Figure 4-7

Place cotton at the scalp

1. Begin at the bottom of one of the back panels; taking ⅛-inch horizontal sections, apply lightener from ½ to one inch away from the scalp to the porous ends. See Figure 4-6.

2. Apply to both sides of each section, progressing to the top of that segment.

3. Between each ⅛-inch section, place a strip of cotton at the scalp. This will help to prevent the lightener from touching the scalp. See Figure 4-7.

4. Move to the other back panel; taking ⅛-inch horizontal sections, apply lightener ½ to one inch away from the scalp, inserting a strip of cotton between each section.

5. Apply to both sides of each section, progressing to the top of the segment.

6. Move to a side segment.

7. Start at the mastoid division line; taking ⅛-inch vertical sections, apply lightener ½ to one inch away from the scalp, inserting a strip of cotton between each section.

Notes

Applying Lightener

continued

Notes

_____
_____
_____
_____
_____
_____
_____
_____
_____
_____
_____
_____
_____
_____
_____
_____
_____
_____
_____
_____
_____
_____
_____
_____
_____
_____
_____

Figure 4-8

Remove cotton

Figure 4-9

Remove cotton

Figure 4-10

Outline segments
with lightener

Figure 4-11

Apply at the scalp

8. Apply to both sides of each section, progressing to the front hairline, laying each vertical section back and away from the face.

9. Repeat Steps 6, 7, and 8 on the other side.

10. Move to the Mohawk segment.

11. Start at the apex; taking ⅛-inch sections, apply lightener ½ to one inch from the scalp, inserting a strip of cotton between each section.

12. Apply to both sides of each section, progressing to the front hairline, laying each section back and away from the face.

13. Lighten to 50–75 percent of the desired result.

14. Move to the back segments and remove the strips of cotton, carefully pulling them out in one direction. See Figure 4-8 and Figure 4-9.

15. Outline the first segment, applying lightener to the scalp. See Figure 4-10.

16. Start at the bottom of the segment and apply the lightener to the scalp, taking ⅛-inch horizontal sections; apply to both sides. See Figure 4-11.

17. Repeat Steps 15 and 16 on the other back segment.

18. Move to the first side panel and remove the strips of cotton, carefully pulling them out in one direction.

19. Outline the side segment, applying lightener to the scalp.

20. Start at the mastoid division line and apply the lightener to the scalp, taking ⅛-inch vertical sections.

21. Apply to both sides, laying each vertical section back and away from the face.

22. Repeat Steps 18, 19, 20, and 21 on the other side segment.

23. Move to the Mohawk segment and remove the strips of cotton, carefully pulling them out in one direction.

Applying Lightener
continued

24. Start at the apex; apply lightener to the scalp, taking ⅛-inch sections.
25. Apply to both sides, laying each section back and away from the face.
26. Process to the desired lightness.
27. Rinse with cool water until all lightener is removed and the water runs clear.
28. Shampoo and condition based on the manufacturer's recommendations.
29. Tone the hair using the product manufacturer's recommendations.

Note: This double-process technique is not designed to replace recommended state board guidelines for virgin and/or retouch lightener applications.

 Watch and listen to the double-process application on Disc One to answer the questions.

Cotton:

1. Why do we use cotton between each section?

   _____

2. How is the cotton removed when it is time to apply lightener to the scalp?

   _____

Timer:

3. What purpose does the timer serve at the end of the double process? _____

4. How much time elapsed during the post-treatment? _____

5. How long did it take to apply the toner? _____

6. After the application of the toner, what was the processing time? _____

7. How much time elapsed during the toner and shampooing? _____

 ## Activity
Using a learning map or windowpane, write the steps for the sectioning and application of double-process color.

✓ Quality Check

After processing the color or lightener, shampooing, conditioning, and styling, it is important to check the quality of your work. With a doll head and on a color service guest, take random horizontal sections throughout the hair.

Figure 4-12

- Are the results even from the scalp through the ends? See Figure 4-12.
- Are there any holidays?
- Is the hairline covered? See Figure 4-13.
- Do you have complete saturation?
- Is the blonde tone consistent throughout?

Figure 4-13

What did you discover? _____

_____

_____

_____

_____

_____

How can you improve next time? _____

_____

_____

_____

_____

_____

Review the skill card for this technique.

Review

1. Where does the application start and why?

   _____

   _____

2. What size of horizontal sections should you take when applying lightener?

   _____

   _____

3. What types of sections are taken starting at the mastoid division line?

   _____

   _____

4. Why do you place a strip of cotton at the scalp when applying lightener?

   _____

   _____

5. What percentage of lightening do you want to see before you apply lightener to the scalp and ends?

   _____

   _____

6. When removing the cotton, what do you want to be careful of?

   _____

   _____

7. Why should you rinse with cool water when working with lightener? How do you know when it is rinsed properly?

   _____

   _____

8. How will you know what to use to tone the hair after using a lightener?

   _____

   _____

9. When and how do you perform a quality check for double-process color?

   _____

   _____

10. In what ways do you protect the porous ends and the scalp during application of double-process color?

    _____

    _____

Platinum Card

The Platinum Card is a unique technique for a double-process application that first decolorizes or lightens the hair and then requires a second application of color to tone the hair into a more desirable color. Although this is a more advanced technique, the use of "back-to-back" foils incubates the hair, which keeps the lightener moist and produces greater results. Always wear gloves when applying lightener and toner.

before

after

Technique Key Points

Watch and listen to the "Technique Key Points — Platinum Card" on Disc One. Circle **True or False**.

1. Section the hair at the bottom of the back of the head. **True   False**

2. Start your application in the front hairline. **True   False**

3. Work from bottom to top. **True   False**

4. Have someone assist you by mixing the lightener. **True   False**

5. Make sure coverage is consistent. **True   False**

6. Make sure there are no holidays. **True   False**

What key points would you add to this list?

_____

_____

Service Area Setup

 Watch and listen to the sanitary maintenance area (SMA) setup in "SMA & Setup" on Disc One to list the basic tools required to begin this technique.

Tools and Equipment

☐ _____
☐ _____
☐ _____
☐ _____
☐ _____
☐ _____
☐ _____
☐ _____
☐ _____
☐ _____
☐ _____

What else do you need to add to this list to stage an extraordinary service experience?

☐ _____
☐ _____
☐ _____
☐ _____
☐ _____
☐ _____
☐ _____
☐ _____
☐ _____

 Review the DVD and skill card for product and tool options.

Diagramming

 Watch and listen to the technique key points for this technique on Disc One. Make note of any additional diagramming tips.

Notes

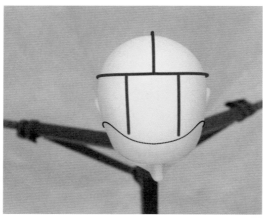

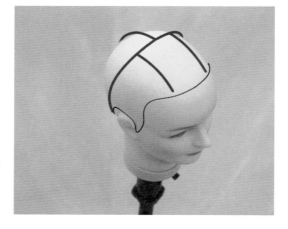

 Activity

On a separate head sheet, practice diagramming this technique.

Parting the Hair for Platinum Card

Figure 4-14

Five segments

Follow these steps for a successful **Platinum Card**, double-process application.

1. Begin parting a mastoid division line from the apex to the mastoid process on both sides, separating the front from the back.

2. Create a vertical part from the apex to the center nape, separating the back into two segments. Clip both segments.

3. In the front segment, create a Mohawk panel by parting the hair using the center of the eye as a guide. Create a horizontal line from the hairline above the eye to the mastoid division line.

4. You will now have five segments. Clip each segment. See Figure 4-14.

Application

Figure 4-15

Apply away from the scalp

1. Begin at the bottom of a back segment, taking ⅛-inch horizontal sections.

2. Place the ⅛-inch foil fold at the base of the scalp, using your hand as a platform to support the foil.

3. Pick up a small amount of lightener with the brush. **TIP:** Wipe any excess product to only one side of the bowl.

4. Apply the lightener ½ to one inch away from the scalp, and then apply through the mid-shaft and ends. **TIP:** Ensure you have thorough saturation without overloading the foil with lightener. See Figure 4-15.

5. Place the brush back into the bowl. **TIP:** Lean the brush to the opposite side of where you wiped any excess product. Doing this will keep the handle of the brush clean.

Refer to Chapter 5 for more information on preparing foils, how to place a foil in the hair, and folding foils.

Notes

Application

continued

Figure 4-16

Completed Platinum Card

Figure 4-17

50–75 percent of desired result

Figure 4-18

Apply at the scalp

6. Using the thumbs, index, and middle fingers on both hands, begin to fold the foil at the middle, so that the bottom end lands even with the top end of the foil. Lightly pinch the fold to secure.

7. Turning the comb vertically even with the width of the section, using the teeth, crease and fold one side of the foil and then the other.

8. Continue foiling back to back, using ⅛-inch horizontal sections, applying the lightener ½ to one inch away from the scalp through the ends until you reach the top of the first back segment.

9. Move to the bottom of the other back segment and mirror each horizontal section as in the first back segment.

10. Go to a side segment.

11. Start at the bottom; take ⅛-inch horizontal sections and continue foiling back to back, progressing to the top of the segment.

12. Move to the other side segment.

13. Starting at the bottom, mirror each horizontal section as in the other side segment.

14. Move to the Mohawk segment.

15. Start at the apex; take ⅛-inch horizontal sections and continue foiling back to back, progressing to the front hairline. See Figure 4-16.

16. Lighten to 50–75 percent of the desired result. See Figure 4-17.

17. Move to the first back segment. **TIP:** Have someone assist you by lifting the foils up.

18. Foil by foil, gently pull the foil just past the line of demarcation.

19. Apply the lightener to the scalp area. See Figure 4-18.

20. Continue working within the same segment sequence as before.

21. Process to the desired lightness.

22. Gently remove each foil and rinse the hair with cool water until all lightener is removed and the water runs clear.

23. Shampoo and condition the hair based on the manufacturer's recommendations.

24. Tone the hair using the product manufacturer's recommendations.

Note: The Platinum Card technique is not designed to replace the recommended state board guidelines for virgin and/or retouch lightener applications.

Activity

Using a learning map or windowpane, write the steps for the sectioning and application for the Platinum Card technique.

Quality Check

After processing the color or lightener, shampooing, conditioning, and styling, it is important to check the quality of your work. With a doll head and on a color service guest, take random horizontal sections throughout the hair.

Figure 4-19

- Are the results even from the scalp through the ends? See Figure 4-19.
- Are there any "holidays"?
- Is the hairline covered? See Figure 4-20.
- Do you have complete saturation?
- Is the blonde tone consistent throughout?

What did you discover? _____
_____
_____
_____
_____

Figure 4-20

How can you improve next time? _____
_____
_____
_____
_____

Review the skill card for this technique.

Review

1. Where does the application start and why?

_____

_____

2. What size of horizontal sections should you take when applying lightener?

_____

3. What types of sections are taken in the back? On the sides?

_____

4. What percentage of desired lightness are you looking for prior to applying at the scalp?

_____

5. How many segments are there?

_____

6. How can you keep the bowl and brush clean throughout the service?

_____

_____

7. Which fingers do you use when folding foil? What are the steps to folding foils?

_____

_____

_____

_____

8. Why should you foil back to back with the Platinum Card technique?

_____

_____

9. When should you go back and apply lightener to the scalp? How should you do that?

_____

_____

10. Why would it be important for you to work in the same segment sequence when applying lightener to the scalp?

_____

_____

Rinsing and Shampooing

The shampoo is every guest's favorite part of a service, but it is especially important when shampooing out hair color. Proper rinsing and shampooing of color is vital to avoid staining the hairline and getting your guest's clothing stained or wet.

 Watch and listen to "Rinsing and Shampooing" on Disc One or Disc Two to fill in the blanks on how to properly rinse and shampoo color.

Figure 4-21

Rinse

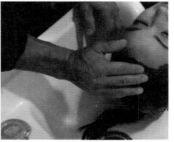

Figure 4-22

Emulsify

Figure 4-23

Lift the head

1. Make sure your guest is _____ _____ and lying _____.

2. Turn on the water using warm water with a _____ _____.

3. Going around the head, wet the hair _____ the _____. See Figure 4-21.

4. Turn the water _____.

5. Using a circular motion, _____ the color around the hairline to _____ any _____. See Figure 4-22.

6. Turn on the water as before; begin to rinse as you continue to _____ the _____ from the _____ and off the _____.

7. Continue _____ _____until the water _____ _____.

8. Turn the _____ off.

9. Using the appropriate _____, work into a _____.

10. Gently lift your guest's head to make sure you _____ behind the _____ and at the _____. See Figure 4-23 .

11. Holding their _____ _____, clean the _____ with a towel.

12. _____ _____ their head back.

13. Turn the _____ on to _____ the shampoo from the hair.

Notes

_____
_____
_____
_____
_____
_____
_____
_____
_____
_____
_____
_____
_____
_____
_____
_____
_____
_____
_____
_____
_____
_____
_____
_____
_____
_____
_____
_____
_____

14. Gently _____ out any excess _____.

15. Apply the appropriate _____ from _____ through _____.

16. As the conditioner sets, give your guest a _____ _____ _____. See Figure 4-24.

17. _____ the conditioner _____.

18. Turn the _____ off and _____ out any _____ water.

19. For _____, _____ a _____ around your guest's head.

Figure 4-24

Massage

20. How do you want your guest to be draped for a shampoo service?

_____

_____

21. What type of water pressure should be used with rinsing and shampooing? _____

_____

22. How do you remove stains from the skin during rinsing and shampooing? _____

_____

23. How will you know that the hair has been rinsed sufficiently?

_____

24. Why is it important to lift the head during rinsing and shampooing?

_____

TIPS:
- Use cool water when rinsing lightener.
- Use warm water at a comfortable temperature when rinsing color.
- Use a gentle water pressure. Full water pressure can force the color into the skin and cause staining.
- To prevent staining around the hairline, rinse the color inside the hairline.
- To ensure you have cleaned behind the ears and at the nape, lift the guest's head to double check.
- Replace wet or soiled towels.

 Activity

Team up with a partner and practice proper rinsing and shampooing color. It is not necessary to have color in the hair. Remember, practice makes perfect!

Quality Check

After rinsing and shampooing the hair, it is important to perform a quality check.

- Has all of the color/lightener been removed?
- Are there stains on the skin or hairline?
- Is the guest dry?
- Has the product been removed from behind the ears and the nape?

What did you discover? _____
_____
_____
_____
_____

How can you improve next time? _____
_____
_____
_____
_____
_____

Activity

Make a Take Home recommendation of shampoo and conditioner for your learning partner using The Wash House menu.

Review

1. Which shampoo would you use after a color service?

   _____

   _____

2. Which shampoo would you use after a lightener service?

   _____

   _____

3. Which conditioner would be best for lightener? For color?

   _____

   _____

4. How do you rinse a panel when the remaining panels have not completed the lightening process?

   _____

   _____

5. Which products would you recommend for your guest to use at home for color? For lightener?

   _____

   _____

6. How do you remove stains from the skin and hairline?

   _____

   _____

7. What can you do to ensure your guest is comfortable during the rinsing and shampooing?

   _____

   _____

8. Which water temperature is used to rinse color? Lightener? Why?

   _____

   _____

9. What might you consider talking to your guest about during the shampoo service?

   _____

   _____

10. What are the steps for giving your guest a relaxing scalp massage? Where do you start? How many repetitions?

   _____

   _____

Learning Review

Read

With each technique, identify what you will focus on to improve your skills.

Reflect

What are some important new skills you have learned? What will you implement in your guest services?

Review

View the DVD and skill cards for each technique. What do you need to improve?

Select/Prioritize

Identify the section and application steps that you need to practice on a doll head. Review your skill cards as you perform the technique.

Draw

On a head sheet, diagram each technique. Windowpane the steps for the application of single process, double process, and Platinum Card.

Share/Act

Teach what you have learned to a friend or coworker.

The Color System

PAUL MITCHELL.
schools

Chapter 5
Foil Work

Everything About Foils and More!

Vertical Slice: Option A—Horseshoe

Vertical Slice: Option B—Boxes

Diagonal Slice: Straight or Curly Hair

Horizontal Weave

Adjusting Flaws

Foil Work

Hair coloring over the years has taken a giant leap forward. Not too long ago, the colorist mostly did one-dimensional, all-over color mainly to cover gray. Or to create dimension, hair was pulled through a rubber cap for a "frosted" effect.

Once used primarily for stage and print work to achieve dramatic effects, foil work began to gain in popularity in the 1980s with new weaving techniques.

The fast-paced 1990s brought demand for more customized services, catapulting the birth of techniques that allowed hair colorists to achieve all-over coverage and dimension in a single process, such as the Paul Mitchell Block Coloring technique.

In the new millennium, guests continue to want a variety of foil work and techniques. The solid basic skill of foil work remains in high demand. This chapter explores the step-by-step techniques for achieving beautiful, head-turning foil work.

 ## Words to Remember

Before you begin, learn the key terms in this chapter. Locate the terms in the glossary.

Apex	Horizontal placement	Section
Bleeding	Lock or locking	Segment
Crown	Mastoid division line	Slice or slicing
Density	Mastoid process	Texture
Diagonal placement	Occipital bone	Vertical placement
Holiday	Panel	Weave or weaving
Horizontal diagonal back	Parietal ridge	Zulu knot

Everything About Foils and More!

Presentation Is Everything!

Proper foil preparation is key for a successful foil weave or slice technique. Well-folded and -placed foils in the hair ensure a clean and beautiful result. Your guests will be impressed when you take extra care in preparing foils and placing them in the hair in a neat and orderly fashion. Because your foil work is so impressive, you will be able to charge more money! Remember, presentation is everything!

About Foil

There are different types of foils available in various weights, colors, and prices. For example:

- Lightweight foil, available in silver only. This foil is often used in restaurants and comes in a box of 750 sheets.

- Boxes of precut 5x5-inch foil. This foil comes in various colors and is available in light, medium, and heavy weights.

- Five-inch width foil rolls. This foil comes in various colors and is available in extra-light, light, medium, and heavy weights.

When using two or three different colors and lightener, using different colored foils can help you to stay organized, knowing which color to place into which foil.

For example:

Place 6N in the blue foil.

Place 7VR in the red foil.

Place lightener in the gold foil.

Preparing Foils

Figure 5-1

Fold ¼ inch

Figure 5-2

Fold in half

1. Tear each foil to an approximate size of 9x5 inches.
2. Fold ¼ inch on one end of the foil. See Figure 5-1.
3. Fold that same ¼ inch in half and crease. You will now have a strong ⅛-inch fold. See Figure 5-2.

Watch and listen to "Foil Prep" on Disc One or Disc Two to answer the questions.

1. How do you prepare the foils for a foil-work service?

_____

2. What is the purpose of this ⅛-inch fold?

_____

How to Place a Foil in the Hair

Figure 5-3

Place the fold at the base

Figure 5-4

Use the hand as a platform

1. Place the ⅛-inch fold at the base of the slice or weave. See Figure 5-3.
2. At the top of the foil, secure the hair and foil with the full length of your thumb.
3. Pick up a small amount of product with the color brush. **TIP:** Wipe any excess product to only one side of the bowl.
4. Begin applying product at the mid-shaft to adhere the hair to the foil.
5. Take the "thumb" hand that was securing the foil and place it under the foil as a "platform." Continue to apply product through the mid-shaft and ends. See Figure 5-4.
6. Move the "platform" hand up to hold the top corners of the foil using the thumb and index finger.

Figure 5-5

Lightly apply at the fold

7. Using any remaining product on the brush, apply the product up to the fold of the foil by lightly "tapping" or "swiping" the product on the hair. See Figure 5-5. **TIP:** "Tapping" the product will help to keep the product off of the scalp and prevent it from bleeding.

8. Keeping the finger and thumb on the top corners of the foil, place the brush back into the bowl. **TIP:** Lean the color brush to the opposite side of where you wiped any excess product. Doing so will keep the handle of the brush clean.

   Note: If you are ***not*** locking the foil, complete Step 9, skip Step 10, and complete Steps 11 and 12. If you are **locking** the foil, skip Step 9; complete Steps 10, 11, and 12; and then continue with the steps for "locking."

Figure 5-6

Fold the foil in half

Figure 5-7

Fold ¼ inch above

Folding Foils

9. Using the thumbs, index, and middle fingers on both hands, begin to fold the foil at the middle so the bottom end lands even with the top end of the foil. Gently pinch the fold to secure. See Figure 5-6.

10. Using the thumbs, index, and middle fingers on both hands, begin to fold the foil at the middle so the bottom end lands about ¼ inch above the top end of the foil, creating a "hood" or "flap." Gently pinch the fold to secure. See Figure 5-7.

11. Using the weave comb, measure from the scalp toward the bottom fold. Wherever the shaft of the comb ends, use the teeth to crease horizontally and fold the foil over the comb. See Figure 5-8.

12. Turning the comb vertically even with the width of the section, using the teeth, crease and fold one side of the foil and then the other. See Figures 5-9 and 5-10.

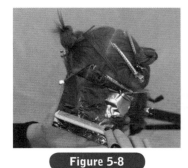

Figure 5-8

Crease and fold horizontally

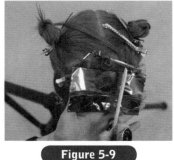

Figure 5-9

Crease and fold

Figure 5-10

Crease and fold

Locking — How to Lock a Foil

Figure 5-11

Gently push with the thumb

In certain areas of the head, it is necessary to "lock" the foils. Those areas are usually the hairline, top of the head, or crown area. This will ensure that the foils won't slide or slip out, allowing the product to touch hair that you don't want it to, causing "bleeding" or "holidays."

TIP: Lock only weaves, not slices.

1. After completing Step 12, using the full length of your thumb placed at the bottom of the foil, gently push the foil packet toward the base. See Figure 5-11.

2. Keeping the foil parallel as you push with your thumb, lay the tail of the comb ¼ inch below the top folded edge of the foil and hold. See Figure 5-12.

3. With the tail of the comb in place holding the foil, fold the packet up and over the tail of the comb.

4. Using your thumb, lightly crease the foil over the tail of the comb. Now, release the foil and the comb. See Figure 5-13.

5. Using both thumbs and index fingers, pinch the top corners (where you just creased the foil) and roll the foil up and toward your body to expose ¼ inch of hair at the base. See Figure 5-14.

6. You will see a foil "flap" at the top of the foil; fold the foil flap to cover the exposed hair. See Figure 5-15.

Congratulations! You have successfully locked a foil!

Figure 5-12

Lay the tail below the edge

Figure 5-13

Fold and crease

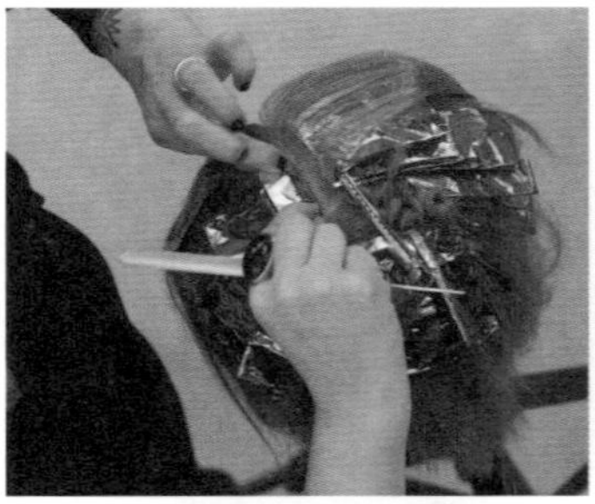

Figure 5-14

Roll the foil at the base

Figure 5-15

Fold to cover the hair

Foiling Tips

1. If a natural look is desired, never foil more than 30–40 percent of the hair.

2. Individual sections are based on hair texture and density.

3. Avoid pulling the foil away from the head by handling the foil lightly.

4. To prevent product from leaking out of the foil, apply the product up to the fold of the foil only.

5. Avoid applying too much product into the foil packets to prevent the foils from swelling or leaking.

6. Try using at least two or three colors to create a more natural look.

7. Know your product and how to formulate. Using the correct product for what you want to achieve is essential.

8. To help the hair adhere to the foil, apply the product to the mid-shaft first and then through the ends. Lightly place minimal product at the top of the foil without going past the fold.

9. Make sure the depth of the weave or slice is fine, no more or less than ⅛-inch. This will help the foil to set closer to the scalp.

10. Develop a good habit of working cleanly and neatly. Presentation is everything!

What tips would you add to this list? _____

_____

_____

_____

_____

_____

_____

Notes

Dropping Foils

Figure 5-16

Once the lightener or color has finished processing, it is time to remove or "drop" the foils from the hair.

1. With the guest double draped and comfortably sitting in The Wash House, begin dropping the foils in the first panel. See Figure 5-16.

2. Starting at the bottom of the panel, carefully unfold and remove each foil one by one until you reach the top of the panel.

3. Continue to the next panel, working in succession.

4. Once all foils are removed, have the guest lie back in the shampoo bowl to begin the rinse and shampoo.

Watch and listen to "Dropping Foils" on Disc One or Disc Two to answer the questions.

1. Where do you begin dropping foils once the color or lightener has processed to the desired results?

   _____

   _____

2. What are the steps to dropping foils?

   _____

   _____

3. What do you do once all foils have been removed?

   _____

   _____

Activity

Practice placing, folding, and dropping 10 foils with a partner.

Review

1. What are the steps for preparing a foil?

   _____

   _____

2. What is the purpose of the fold in the foil?

   _____

   _____

3. What are the steps for placing a foil in the hair?

   _____

   _____

   _____

   _____

4. What is the purpose of the thumb when foiling?

   _____

   _____

5. What is referred to as a "platform" when foiling?

   _____

   _____

6. How do you lock a foil?

   _____

   _____

   _____

   _____

7. What is the purpose for locking a foil?

   _____

   _____

8. Do you lock a foil on a weave or a slice?

   _____

9. On what areas of the head is it recommended to lock the foils?

   _____

10. When folding the foil packet, what is the difference in folding when locking versus not locking?

    _____

    _____

Vertical Slice
Option A—Horseshoe

This vertical slice option can be done on straight or curly hair and features easy parting and a flowing application process. A slice is a "slither" of hair color and appears stronger than a weave because more hair is colored. A bolder or stripy look can be achieved by placing back-to-back foils. Vertical color placement works well with layered haircuts. Slices can be done on hair that is at least three inches in length or longer.

before

after

Technique Key Points

Watch and listen to "Technique Key Points: Vertical Slice—Option A" on Disc One. Number the steps in the proper order.

_____ Use your hand as a platform.

_____ Take ¼-inch sections.

_____ Skim off the top.

_____ Check the length of your layers.

_____ Create your zigzag.

_____ Apply at the mid-shaft.

_____ Make sure slices are consistent.

_____ Create your horseshoe or horseshoes.

_____ Presentation is everything; keep your foils neat.

_____ Make sure you have covered 30–40 percent of the hair.

_____ For a natural result, take a fine section of hair around the hairline and drop it out.

What key points would you add to this list?

_____

_____

Notes

_____

Service Area Setup

 Watch and listen to the sanitary maintenance area (SMA) setup in "SMA & Setup" on Disc One to list the basic tools required to begin this technique.

Tools and Equipment

☐ _____

☐ _____

☐ _____

☐ _____

☐ _____

☐ _____

☐ _____

☐ _____

☐ _____

☐ _____

What else do you need to add to this list to stage an extraordinary service experience?

☐ _____

☐ _____

☐ _____

☐ _____

☐ _____

☐ _____

☐ _____

☐ _____

☐ _____

  Review the DVD and skill card for product and tool options.

Diagramming

Watch and listen to the technique key points for this technique on Disc One.
Make note of any additional diagramming tips.

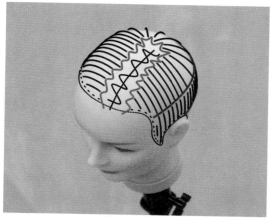

Notes

_____

_____

_____

_____

_____

_____

_____

_____

_____

_____

_____

_____

_____

_____

_____

_____

_____

_____

_____

_____

_____

_____

_____

_____

Activity

On a separate head sheet, practice diagramming this technique.

Sectioning the Hair

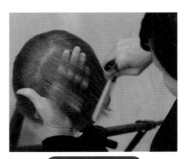

Figure 5-17

Check for consistency

Figure 5-18

Create a zigzag part

Figure 5-19

Create a horizontal parting

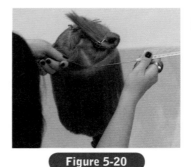

Figure 5-20

Create a horizontal parting

Optional — **Before you begin:** For wavy, curly, and extra-curly hair, you may blow-dry the hair as straight as possible for ease in the parting and application portion. Blow-drying the hair before applying the foils will maintain consistent parting and foiling application.

1. Begin by finding the natural part. Comb the hair from the front hairline to the crown. **TIP:** Press on the crown with the palm of your hand. As the hair falls, it will automatically "split" or separate into its natural part. Do this two or three times to confirm where the natural part is.

2. Create a zigzag on one side of the natural part.
   TIP: The depth of the zigzag is determined by the texture of the hair. On finer hair, the zigzag will have more depth; on coarser hair, it will have less depth.

3. Place the hair on the back or palm of your hand to check for consistency and desired visibility. Seeing directly through to your hand may mean that you will see stripes. Adjust accordingly. Clip the zigzag. See Figure 5-17.

4. Create a zigzag on the other side of the natural part, checking for consistency. Clip the two zigzags together. See Figure 5-18.

5. Create a third zigzag at the crown, connecting the two existing zigzags. Check for consistency.

6. Combine the three zigzags into one segment, twist into a Zulu knot, and clip.

7. Beginning on either side of the natural part at the front hairline, create a horizontal parting along the lower parietal ridge to just behind the ear. Create a vertical parting, also known as the *mastoid division line,* from the zigzag connecting to the horizontal line. Twist this segment into a Zulu knot and clip. See Figure 5-19.

8. Continue the horizontal parting through the lower part of the crown to just behind the ear on the other side. Create a vertical parting, also known as the *mastoid division line,* from the zigzag to meet the horizontal line. Twist this segment into a Zulu knot and clip. See Figure 5-20.

Sectioning the Hair

continued

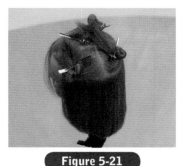

Figure 5-21

Mirror the first segment

9. The third segment mirrors the first segment on the opposite side. Twist into a Zulu knot and clip. You now have a three-segment horseshoe. **TIP:** Based on the length of the layers or the degree of graduation, a second horseshoe segment may be necessary; if so, proceed to Step 10. See Figure 5-21.

10. Beginning on either side just above the ear in the front hairline, create a horizontal parting along the lower temporal to just behind the ear. Create a vertical parting, also known as the *mastoid division line,* from the upper horseshoe connecting to the horizontal parting. Twist this panel into a Zulu knot and clip.

11. Continue the horizontal parting through the occipital region to just behind the ear on the other side. Create a vertical parting, also known as the *mastoid division line,* from the upper horseshoe connecting to the horizontal parting. Twist this panel into a Zulu knot and clip.

12. The third panel mirrors the first panel on the opposite side. Twist into a Zulu knot and clip. You now have two (2) three-panel horseshoes to foil.

Notes

Activity

By rearranging the sectioning steps for a vertical slice, see if you can accomplish the same pattern and number of panels.

1. By rearranging the steps, where did you begin the sections?
2. What did you discover?

Vertical Slice and Foil Placement

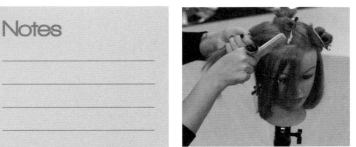

Figure 5-22

Begin behind the hairline

Figure 5-23

Slice off the top

Figure 5-24

Measure ¼ inch

Figure 5-25

Completed vertical slice

Before you begin: If there are two horseshoe panels, begin foiling in the lower panel. Finish the lower panel from one side to the other before moving to the upper horseshoe panels.

1. Begin the vertical slice on the side you are most comfortable working.

2. To avoid stripes or dots in the hairline, first section and clip the hairline out. The depth of this section depends on the hair density at the hairline.

3. Begin with a vertical section directly behind the hairline section. **TIP:** To ensure your sections are vertical, stand directly even with each section. See Figure 5-22.

4. Take a ¼-inch vertical section. Clip the rest of the panel for control.

5. From the ¼-inch vertical section, take a "slice" off of the top of that same section. See Figure 5-23.

TIP: For better control and organization, clip hair that you are not foiling out of the way.

6. To continue, follow the steps for "How to Place a Foil in the Hair."

7. **Note:** When placing foils through the upper crown panel, due to the roundness of the crown, the sections will be more narrow at the top and wider at the bottom of this panel. You will need to measure each vertical section ¼ inch at the top of the panel. See Figure 5-24.

8. Continue foiling vertically throughout each panel from one side to the other side. See Figure 5-25.

TIP: Make sure to leave out the front hairline to mirror the other side.

✓ Quality Check

After processing the color or lightener, shampooing, conditioning, and then styling the hair, it is important to check the quality of your work.

When checking the color on a guest or doll head, brush the hair away from the face as well as brush the hair in different directions to view the vertical slices.

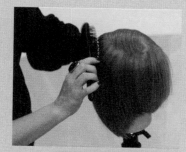

Figure 5-26

Check for the following (see Figure 5-26):
- Are the slices the same size?
- Is the space between each slice the same?
- Are the slices consistent throughout?
- Are the slices vertical?
- Is the total amount colored 30–40 percent of the hair?
- Is 60–70 percent of the hair still natural?
- Is the end result even from the scalp through the ends?
- Can you see the slices of color peeking through to the natural part without being "stripy"?
- Do you see stripes or dots around the hairline? See Figure 5-27.

Figure 5-27

What did you discover? _____
_____
_____
_____

How can you improve next time? _____
_____
_____
_____

Review the skill card for this technique.

◉ Review

1. What look does the horseshoe vertical slice give you?

    _____

    _____

2. How do you determine if you need two horseshoes?

    _____

    _____

3. If there are two horseshoes, which horseshoe do you foil first?

    _____

    _____

4. Where do you begin the vertical slices?

    _____

    _____

5. How do you ensure that your slices are vertical?

    _____

    _____

6. Why is it important to section the hairline out?

    _____

    _____

7. What determines the depth of the zigzags?

    _____

    _____

8. Where do you begin sectioning for horseshoe vertical slice?

    _____

    _____

9. Where do you begin foiling in horseshoes?

    _____

    _____

10. How do you create a bolder slice?

    _____

    _____

Vertical Slice
Option B—Boxes

This vertical slice using boxes maintains a vertical line within the shape, creates organization for a quick application process, and can be used on straight or curly hair. Slices are ideal for medium to coarse hair texture when a weave would not be seen and can be done on hair that is at least three inches in length or longer. Vertical color placement works well with layered haircuts.

before

after

Technique Key Points

 Watch and listen to "Technique Key Points: Vertical Slice—Option B" on Disc One. Circle True or False.

1 Create your zigzag. **True   False**

2 Create your segments. **True   False**

3 Take ½-inch sections. **True   False**

4 Skim off the bottom. **True   False**

5 Apply at the mid-shaft. **True   False**

6 Use your hand as a platform. **True   False**

7 Presentation is everything; keep your color organized. **True   False**

8 Make sure your slices are consistent. **True   False**

9 Make sure you have covered 50–60 percent of the hair. **True   False**

What key points would you add to this list?

_____

_____

Service Area Setup

 Watch and listen to the sanitary maintenance area (SMA) setup in "SMA & Setup" on Disc One to list the basic tools required to begin this technique.

Tools and Equipment

☐ _____

☐ _____

☐ _____

☐ _____

☐ _____

☐ _____

☐ _____

☐ _____

☐ _____

☐ _____

☐ _____

What else do you need to add to this list to stage an extraordinary service experience?

☐ _____

☐ _____

☐ _____

☐ _____

☐ _____

☐ _____

☐ _____

☐ _____

☐ _____

  Review the DVD and skill card for product and tool options.

Diagramming

 Watch and listen to the technique key points for this technique on Disc One. Make note of any additional diagramming tips.

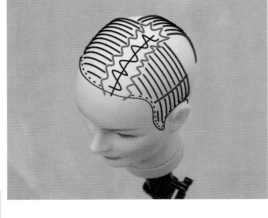

 ## Activity

On a separate head sheet, practice diagramming this technique.

Sectioning the Hair

Figure 5-28

First side segment

***Optional* — Before you begin:** For wavy, curly, and extra-curly hair, you may blow-dry the hair as straight as possible for ease in the parting and application portion. Blow-drying the hair before applying the foils maintains consistent parting and foiling application.

1. Begin by finding the natural part. Comb the hair from the front hairline to the crown. **TIP:** Press on the crown with the palm of your hand. As the hair falls, it will automatically "split" or separate into its natural part. Do this two or three times to confirm where the natural part is.

2. Create a zigzag on one side of the natural part.
   TIP: The depth of the zigzag is determined by the texture of the hair. On finer hair, the zigzag will have more depth; on coarser hair, it will have less depth.

3. Place the hair on the back or palm of your hand to check for consistency and desired visibility. Seeing directly through to your hand may mean that you will see stripes. Adjust accordingly. Clip this zigzag.

4. Create a zigzag on the other side of the natural part, checking for consistency. Clip the two zigzags together.

5. Create a third zigzag at the crown, connecting the two existing zigzags. Check for consistency.

6. Combine the three zigzags into one segment, twist into a Zulu knot, and clip.

7. Beginning on either side of the natural part at the front hairline, create a horizontal parting along the lower parietal ridge to just behind the ear. Create a vertical parting, also known as the *mastoid division line,* from the zigzag connecting to the horizontal line. Twist this segment into a Zulu knot and clip. See Figure 5-28.

8. Mirror on the other side by parting horizontally along the lower parietal ridge to the mastoid division line. Create a vertical part from the zigzag segment down the mastoid division line meeting the horizontal part. Twist into a Zulu knot and clip. **Note:** This side panel will be larger than the other side panel since it is furthest from the natural part.

9. Move to the back of the zigzag near the crown; part a vertical line from one side of the zigzag down to the occipital.

10. Repeat on the other side of the zigzag by parting a vertical line down to the occipital.

Sectioning the Hair

continued

Figure 5-29

Back segment

Figure 5-30

Mirror on the other side

Figure 5-31

Lower side "box"

Figure 5-32

Completed panels

11. Part a horizontal line across the occipital, connecting the two vertical lines. Twist into a Zulu knot and clip. You will now have three separate segments or "boxes." See Figure 5-29.

TIP: Based on the length of the layers or the degree of graduation, three lower panels or boxes may be necessary; if so, proceed to Step 12.

12. Return to the first side; from the hairline, create a horizontal parting along the lower temporal to the mastoid division line. Part vertically down the mastoid division line, meeting the horizontal line. Twist this panel into a Zulu knot and clip. See Figure 5-30.

13. Mirror on the other side by parting horizontally along the lower temporal to the mastoid division line. Continue the vertical part down the mastoid division line to meet the horizontal part. Twist into a Zulu knot and clip. See Figure 5-31.

14. Move to the back and create a panel directly under the first back panel by continuing both vertical lines, connecting them with a horizontal line along the lower occipital. Twist into a Zulu knot and clip. You will now have a total of six panels to foil. See Figure 5-32.

Activity

By rearranging the sectioning steps for a vertical slice, see if you can accomplish the same pattern and number of panels.

1. When rearranging the steps, where did you begin the sections?
2. What did you discover?

Vertical Slice and Foil Placement

Notes

Figure 5-33

Drop the hairline

Figure 5-34

Foil to the other side

Figure 5-35

Completed vertical slice

TIP: If there are six panels, begin foiling in the lower three panels. Finish the lower three panels from one side to the other before moving to the upper three panels.

1. Begin the vertical slice on the side you are most comfortable working.

2. To avoid stripes or dots in the hairline, first section and clip the hairline out. The depth of this section depends on the density of the hairline. See Figure 5-33.

3. Begin with a vertical section directly behind the hairline section. **TIP:** To ensure your sections are vertical, stand even with each section.

4. Take a ¼-inch vertical section. Clip the rest of the panel for control.

5. From the ¼-inch vertical section, take a "slice" off of the top of that same section. **TIP:** For better control and organization, clip hair that you are not foiling out of the way.

6. To continue, follow the steps for "How to Place a Foil in the Hair."

7. Continue foiling vertically throughout each lower panel to the other side. Make sure to leave out the front hairline to mirror the other side. See Figure 5-34.

8. Once the lower panels are completed, move to the top panels. See Figure 5-35.

Quality Check

After processing the color or lightener, shampooing, conditioning, and then styling the hair, it is important to check the quality of your work.

When checking the color on a guest or doll head, brush the hair away from the face as well as brush the hair in different directions to view the vertical slices.

Check for the following:

- Are the slices the same size?
- Is the space between each slice the same?
- Are the slices consistent throughout?
- Are the slices vertical? See Figure 5-36.
- Is the total amount colored 30–40 percent of the hair?
- Is 60–70 percent of the hair still natural?
- Is the end result even from the scalp through the ends?

Figure 5-36

- Can you see the slices of color peeking through to the natural part without being "stripy"?
- Do you see stripes or dots around the hairline?

What did you discover? _____

_____

_____

_____

_____

How can you improve next time? _____

_____

_____

_____

_____

 Review the skill card for this technique.

Review

1. Slices are ideal for what texture and formations of hair?

   _____

   _____

2. When do you use only three boxes?

   _____

   _____

3. How do you determine if you need six boxes?

   _____

   _____

4. If there are six boxes, where do you begin the vertical slices?

   _____

   _____

5. Why is it important to section the hairline out?

   _____

   _____

6. Where do you begin foiling in boxes?

   _____

   _____

7. What do you do with the hairline in a vertical slice?

   _____

   _____

8. What effect does a vertical placement create?

   _____

   _____

9. When slicing, what percentage of hair is colored?

   _____

   _____

10. What size should each section be for a slice? And then what do you do?

    _____

    _____

Diagonal Slice
Straight or Curly Hair

A diagonal slice placement can be performed on straight **(red numbers)** or curly hair **(blue numbers)** when the hair is at least three inches in length or longer. It is best suited on medium to coarse hair textures and is great for curly and darker levels when a weave would not be seen. The effect of a slice is stronger than a weave because more hair is used. Diagonal color placement works well with graduation.

The diagonal slice has been demonstrated on two different models and doll heads, each with different hair textures and formation.

before

after

before

after

Technique Key Points

Watch and listen to "Technique Key Points: Diagonal Slice" on Disc One to fill in the blanks.

1 Start your _____ at the _____.

2 Check the _____ _____ at the back.

3 Ensure you have a _____ _____ _____ parting.

4 Take _____-inch sections.

5 Skim off the _____.

6 Apply at the _____.

7 Use your hand as a _____.

8 _____ is everything; keep your _____ neat.

9 Make sure _____ are consistent.

10 Make sure you have covered _____ to _____ percent of the hair.

What key points would you add to this list?

_____

_____

Notes

_____

_____

_____

_____

_____

_____

_____

_____

_____

_____

_____

_____

_____

_____

_____

_____

_____

_____

_____

_____

_____

_____

_____

_____

_____

_____

_____

_____

_____

_____

Service Area Setup

 Watch and listen to the sanitary maintenance area (SMA) setup in "SMA & Setup" on Disc One to list the basic tools required to begin this technique.

Tools and Equipment

☐ _____

☐ _____

☐ _____

☐ _____

☐ _____

☐ _____

☐ _____

☐ _____

☐ _____

☐ _____

☐ _____

What else do you need to add to this list to stage an extraordinary service experience?

☐ _____

☐ _____

☐ _____

☐ _____

☐ _____

☐ _____

☐ _____

☐ _____

☐ _____

   Review the DVD and skill card for product and tool options.

Diagramming

 Watch and listen to the technique key points for this technique on Disc One. Make note of any additional diagramming tips.

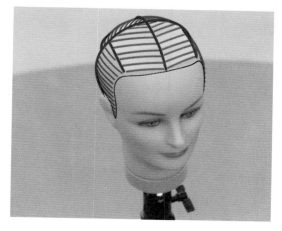

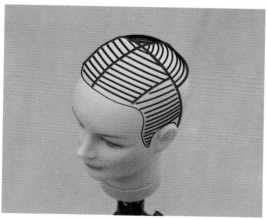

Activity

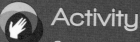

On a separate head sheet, practice diagramming this technique.

Sectioning the Hair

Figure 5-37

Create a center part

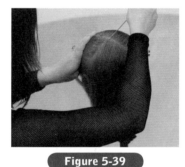

Figure 5-39

Create a mastoid division line

Figure 5-41

Mastoid division line

Figure 5-43

Create two panels

Optional — **Before you begin:** For wavy, curly, and extra-curly hair, you may blow-dry the hair as straight as possible for ease in the parting and application portion. Blow-drying the hair before applying the foils maintains consistent parting and foiling application.

1. Begin with a center part from the front hairline to the apex. See Figures 5-37 and 5-38.

2. From the apex, part a mastoid division line to the mastoid process. Separate and clip the front segment from the back segment. See Figures 5-39 and 5-40.

3. Mirror on the other side by parting the mastoid division line from the apex to the mastoid process. Separate and clip the front segment from the back segment. See Figure 5-41 and 5-42.

4. On one front side, at the natural recession, part along the parietal to the mastoid division line. Twist each panel into a Zulu knot and clip. See Figures 5-43 and 5-44.

Figure 5-38

Create a center part

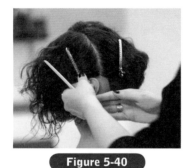

Figure 5-40

Create a mastoid division line

Figure 5-42

Mastoid division line

Figure 5-44

Create two panels

Sectioning the Hair

continued

Figure 5-45
Create two panels

Figure 5-47
Checking graduation

Figure 5-49
Horizontal-diagonal-back parting

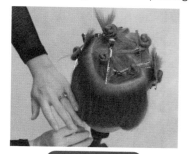

Figure 5-51
Completed panels

5. Mirror on the other side, parting at the natural recession along the parietal to the mastoid division line. Twist each panel into a Zulu knot and clip. See Figures 5-45 and 5-46.

6. Continue the center part from the apex to the greater occipital or to the weight of the graduation. See Figure 5-47.

Checking Graduation Tip: If the hair has not been precut, continue the center part to the nape. See Figure 5-48.

7. From the vertical center part at the greater occipital, part a horizontal-diagonal-back line to both mastoid division lines. (See the tip below.) See Figures 5-49 and 5-50. Twist each back panel into a Zulu knot and clip.

8. You will have six panels. See Figures 5-51 and 5-52.

TIP: To see the slices better on a curly or extra-curly formation, take a deeper "chevron" section or diagonal back sections.

Figure 5-46
Create two panels

Figure 5-48
Continue the part to the nape

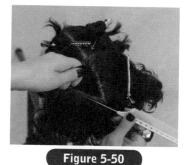

Figure 5-50
Horizontal-diagonal-back parting

Figure 5-52
Completed panels

Diagonal Slice and Foil Placement

Figure 5-53

First foil placement

1. Begin in either back panel. Part a ¼-inch section mirroring the horizontal-diagonal-back section along the bottom of the panel. See Figures 5-53 and 5-54. **TIP:** If the section is wider than two inches due to the roundness of the head, split the section in half and place two foils side by side.

2. From the ¼-inch horizontal-diagonal-back section, part a **"slice"** off of the top of that same section.

3. To continue, follow the steps for "How to Place a Foil in the Hair" and "Locking — How to Lock a Foil."

4. Continue **slicing** and foiling up to the crown, stopping two foils short of the top of the back panel.

5. Because of growth patterns in the crown and to prevent "stripes" peeking through, the last two panels must be **weaved**. See Figures 5-55 and 5-56. **TIP:** It is recommended to lock these two foils at the crown. Follow the steps for locking.

6. Repeat Steps 1–5 on the other back panel.

7. Move to either side panel to start at the bottom. See Figure 5-57. To avoid "stripes" in the sideburn area, **weave** and foil **two** (2) ⅛-inch sections at a horizontal-diagonal-back angle. See Figure 5-58. **TIP:** It is recommended to lock these two foils at the hairline.

Figure 5-54

First slice

Figure 5-55

Weave near the crown

Figure 5-56

Weave near the crown

Figure 5-58

Weaving at the hairline

Figure 5-57

Move to the bottom side

Diagonal Slice and Foil Placement
Continued

Figure 5-59

Continue with slicing

Figure 5-61

Weave at the hairline

Figure 5-63

Continue with slicing

Figure 5-65

Completed diagonal slice

8. Return to slicing on the third foil, parting in ¼-inch horizontal-diagonal-back sections. Continue to the top of this panel. See Figures 5-59 and 5-60.

9. Move to the other side panel and repeat Steps 6, 7, and 8.

10. Standing in front of the guest, move to either top panel. To avoid a heavy line or "stripe" at the hairline, **weave** and foil two (2) ⅛-inch sections. See Figures 5-61 and 5-62.

TIP: It is recommended to lock the foils at the hairline. (**Note:** To maintain consistency, the spaces between the weaves must match the distance between the slices on the lower side panels.)

11. Return to **slicing** on the third foil, parting in ¼-inch diagonal sections. See Figure 5-63. Continue **slicing** and foiling, stopping two foils short of the end of the panel near the crown.

12. Because of growth patterns in the crown and to prevent "stripes" peeking through, the last two panels must be **weaved**. See Figure 5-64. **TIP:** It is recommended to lock these last foils at the crown.

13. Standing in front of the guest, move to the other top panel and repeat Steps 10, 11, and 12.

Figure 5-60

Continue with slicing

Figure 5-62

Weave at the hairline

Figure 5-64

Weave at the crown

Notes

✓ Quality Check

Figure 5-66

Figure 5-67

After processing the color or lightener, shampooing, conditioning, and styling, it is important to check the quality of your work.

With a doll head, you have the luxury of turning the doll head upside down to check the diagonal slice. See Figures 5-66 and 5-67.

When checking the color on a service guest, brush the hair away from the face and in different directions to allow you to view the results throughout.

Check for the following:

- Are the slices the same size? See Figure 5-68.
- Is the space between each slice the same?
- Are the slices consistent throughout? See Figure 5-69.
- Are the slices diagonal?
- Is the total amount colored 30–40 percent of the hair?
- Is 60–70 percent of the hair still natural?
- Is the end result even from the scalp through the ends?
- Do you see stripes or dots around the hairline? See Figures 5-70 and 5-71.
- Do the slices fall even with the graduation? See Figure 5-72.

Figure 5-68

Figure 5-70

Figure 5-69

Figure 5-71

Figure 5-72

What did you discover? _____
_____
_____
_____
_____

How can you improve next time? _____
_____
_____
_____
_____

Review the skill card for this technique.

Review

1. Where do you begin sectioning for a diagonal slice?

   _____

   _____

2. Where do you begin foiling on a diagonal slice?

   _____

   _____

3. Diagonal placement works well with what type of haircut?

   _____

   _____

4. What do you do if you want to achieve a bolder slice?

   _____

   _____

5. What effect does a diagonal placement create?

   _____

   _____

6. When slicing, what percentage of hair is colored?

   _____

   _____

7. What size should each section be for a slice? And then what do you do?

   _____

   _____

8. Where do you weave the hair when performing a slice technique?

   _____

   _____

9. When weaving in the sideburn area, what size should each section be?

   _____

   _____

10. How is horizontal, vertical, and diagonal placement related to block coloring?

    _____

    _____

Horizontal Weave
Straight Hair

When weaving a guest's hair, taking into consideration the texture and formation of the hair is essential. There is no "right" or "wrong" size or space of the weave, but know that a finer weave creates a softer or more natural result and a chunkier weave creates a heavier or bolder result. To determine whether to perform a finer weave or chunkier weave, it is important to understand the guest's desired result.

Just as we have a pattern for sectioning, we also have a pattern for weaving. This helps you to reproduce the weave each time your guests return for their service. It is recommended that you take evenly spaced weaves that are consistent throughout. Whatever you select as a weave requires double the space between each "ribbon" or weave.

Horizontal color placement works well with one-length haircuts. Weaves are like "fine ribbons of hair," can give a natural dimensional color effect, and can be performed on hair that is at least three inches in length or longer.

after

before

Technique Key Points

Watch and listen to "Technique Key Points — Horizontal Weave" on Disc One. Number the steps in the proper order.

_____ Weave using a one-to-two ratio.

_____ Make sure weaves are consistent.

_____ Divide the front and back segments.

_____ Apply at the mid-shaft.

_____ Make sure you have no bleeding or holidays.

_____ Start your weave in the back.

_____ Create a Mohawk panel.

_____ Use your hand as a platform.

_____ Zulu knot and clip.

_____ Lock where appropriate.

_____ Make sure you have covered 30–40 percent of the hair.

What key points would you add to this list?

_____

_____

Weaving Tips

- When weaving, it is recommended to pick up the hair at the front hairline with each section.

- When there are foils setting side by side, continue the "weaving" pattern from one foil into the neighboring foil. For example: If you end with a weave or "ribbon" of hair in a foil, make sure to leave a space before a weave or ribbon within the neighboring foil. Or if you end with a space in a foil, make sure to begin with a weave or ribbon in the neighboring foil. This will create consistency and ensure you don't have two weaves or two spaces next to each other.

Service Area Setup

Watch and listen to the sanitary maintenance area (SMA) setup in "SMA & Setup" on Disc One to list the basic tools required to begin this technique.

Tools and Equipment

☐ _____
☐ _____
☐ _____
☐ _____
☐ _____
☐ _____
☐ _____
☐ _____
☐ _____
☐ _____
☐ _____

What else do you need to add to this list to stage an extraordinary service experience?

☐ _____
☐ _____
☐ _____
☐ _____
☐ _____
☐ _____
☐ _____
☐ _____
☐ _____

Review the DVD and skill card for product and tool options.

Diagramming

 Watch and listen to the technique key points for this technique on Disc One. Make note of any additional diagramming tips.

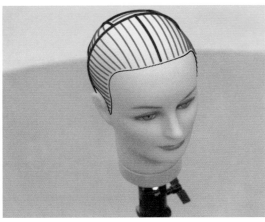

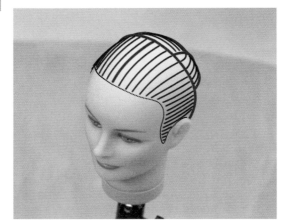

 ## Activity

On a separate head sheet, practice diagramming this technique.

Sectioning the Hair

Figure 5-73

Mastoid division line

Figure 5-74

Mastoid division line

Figure 5-75

Part horizontally

Figure 5-76

Create three panels

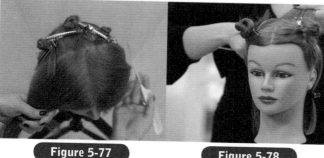

Figure 5-77

Create a center part

Figure 5-78

Create a center part

Figure 5-79

Create a small "box"

1. Begin with a mastoid division line from the apex to the mastoid process; separate and clip the front segment from the back segment. See Figure 5-73.

2. Mirror on the other side by parting a mastoid division line from the apex to the mastoid process; separate and clip the front segment from the back segment. See Figure 5-74.

3. From the mastoid division line, part horizontally across the greater occipital to the mastoid division line on the other side. See Figure 5-75.

4. At the mastoid division line on either side of the apex, part a two-inch wide Mohawk panel connecting to the horizontal line at the occipital. Twist all three back panels into Zulu knots and clip. See Figure 5-76.

5. Part a center part from the apex to the front hairline. Twist each panel into a Zulu knot and clip. See Figures 5-77 and 5-78.

6. Two inches below the apex within the Mohawk panel, part a horizontal section across the crown, creating a small "box." Twist into a Zulu knot and clip. See Figure 5-79.

Activity

By rearranging the sectioning steps for a horizontal weave, see if you can accomplish the same pattern and number of panels.
1. By rearranging the steps, where did you begin the sections?
2. What did you discover?

Horizontal Weave and Foil Placement

Figure 5-80

Begin in the Mohawk panel

1. Begin the weave in the back at the bottom of the Mohawk panel. Part a ¼-inch horizontal section. See Figure 5-80. **TIP:** For better control, clip the rest of the section up.

2. Divide the ¼-inch horizontal section in half and drop the bottom half.

3. **"Weave"** off the top section using the tip of the tail of the comb in and out of this ⅛-inch section. **Weave** evenly, making sure there is double the space between each "ribbon" or weave.

TIP: Consistency in the weave technique ensures the ability to reproduce the same results the next time the guest returns.

4. To continue, follow the steps for "How to Place a Foil in the Hair."

5. Continue **weaving** and foiling to the top of this back Mohawk panel.

Figure 5-81

Weave ⅛-inch sections

6. Move to either sideburn area and weave two (2) fine, ⅛-inch horizontal sections. See Figure 5-81.
   TIP: Include the hairline in the **weave** to avoid a "shadow" around the face. **TIP:** It is recommended to lock these first two foils.

7. To continue, follow the steps for "Locking — How to Lock a Foil."

Figure 5-82

Even with back panel

Figure 5-83

Foil side by side

8. Return to ¼-inch sections on the third foil, divide the section in half, drop the bottom half, and weave the top section. **TIP:** Include the hairline in the weave.

9. Continue weaving and foiling until even with the side back panel. See Figure 5-82.

10. Begin to alternate foiling within the side back panel and the front panel, placing the foils side by side. See Figure 5-83. Continue to the center part. **TIP:** It is recommended to lock the last two rows of foils at the center part.

11. Repeat Steps 6, 7, 8, 9, and 10 on the other side. See Figure 5-84.

12. Move to the "box" panel in the crown; begin weaving in the front of the panel, so the foils lie forward. See Figure 5-85.
 TIP: It is recommended to lock these foils.

Figure 5-84

Completed back, side, and top panels

Figure 5-85

Weave "box" panel last

Activity

Using a windowpane or learning map, review all of the steps for sectioning and weaving for the horizontal weave.

Quality Check

After processing the color or lightener, shampooing, conditioning, then styling the hair, it is important to check the quality of your work.

With a doll head, you have the luxury of turning the doll head upside down to check the horizontal weave. See Figure 5-86.

Figure 5-86

When checking the color on a service guest, brush the hair away from the face and in different directions to view the horizontal weave.

Check for the following (see Figures 5-87 and 5-88):

- Are the weaves the same size?
- Is the space between each weave double the size of the weave?
- Are the sections consistent throughout?
- Are the weaves horizontal?
- Is the total amount colored 30–40 percent of the hair?
- Is 60–70 percent of the hair still natural?
- Is the end result even from the scalp through the ends?
- Do you see shadows around the hairline or does the weave blend in?

Figure 5-87

Figure 5-88

What did you discover? _____

_____

_____

How can you improve next time? _____

_____

_____

Review the skill card for this technique.

Review

1. Where do you begin sectioning for a horizontal weave?

   _____

   _____

2. Horizontal placement works well with what type of haircut?

   _____

   _____

3. What effect does a horizontal placement create?

   _____

   _____

4. Where do you begin foiling on a horizontal weave?

   _____

   _____

5. What is the last panel completed on a horizontal weave?

   _____

   _____

6. When weaving, what percentage of hair is colored?

   _____

   _____

7. What size should each section be for a weave? And then what do you do?

   _____

   _____

8. When performing a horizontal weave, what do you do with the front hairline?

   _____

   _____

9. When weaving in the sideburn area, what size should each section be?

   _____

   _____

10. What type of effect does a weave give?

   _____

   _____

Adjusting Flaws

While performing a quality check, you may discover a flaw, such as:

1. Strands of hair within a weave or slice are too heavy or too bold. See Figure 5-89.

2. Too much color or lightener was applied, resulting in product leaking from the foil, causing bleeding or a hot spot. See Figure 5-90.

3. The color or lightener was applied too far from the fold of the foil, resulting in a holiday. See Figure 5-91.

It is easy to adjust any flaw; just follow these simple steps for a "flawless" end result!

Figure 5-89

Heavy weave

Figure 5-90

Hot spot

Figure 5-91

Holiday

How to Adjust a Heavy Weave or Slice

1. Begin by isolating the "heavy" or "bold" strands to create the same sized section of the weave or slice as before. See Figure 5-92.

2. Mix the color to match the desired end result.

3. Place the strands in a foil and apply the color. See Figure 5-93.

4. Fold the foil and process.

Figure 5-92

Isolate strands

Figure 5-93

Apply color

How to Adjust Bleeding or a Hot Spot

Figure 5-94

Isolate hot spot

Figure 5-95

Apply color

Figure 5-96

Process color

1. To ensure that you adjust only the affected areas, isolate the "hot spot" by taking fine sections. See Figure 5-94.

2. Take a two- to three-inch strip of cotton and tear it lengthwise into two to four smaller strips.

3. Mix the color to match the desired end result.

4. Place a cotton strip underneath the "hot spot" that must be adjusted and apply the color. See Figure 5-95.

5. Place a second strip of cotton directly on the top and process. See Figure 5-96.

Notes

How to Adjust a Holiday

Figure 5-97

Isolate holiday

Figure 5-98

Apply product

Figure 5-99

Process color

1. To ensure that you adjust only the affected areas, isolate the "holiday" by taking fine sections. See Figure 5-97.

2. Take a two- to three-inch strip of cotton and tear it lengthwise into two to four smaller strips.

3. Mix the product to match the desired end result.

4. Place a cotton strip underneath the "holiday" that must be adjusted and apply the product. See Figure 5-98.

5. Place a second strip of cotton directly on the top and process. See Figure 5-99.

Activity

Practice each of the flaw adjustments.

✓ Quality Check

After processing the color or lightener, shampooing, conditioning, and styling, it is important to check the quality of your work. With a doll head and on a color service guest, return to the quality check for the technique you performed and recheck your work.

Were you successful in adjusting any flaws? _____
_____
_____
_____

Did you create any new flaws? _____
_____
_____
_____

What did you discover? _____
_____
_____
_____

What can you do to prevent flaws in future color services? _____
_____
_____
_____

Review

1. What tools do you need to begin a flaw adjustment?

    _____

    _____

2. How do flaw adjustment applications differ from the original application process?

    _____

    _____

3. When during the color or lightener service might you discover flaws?

    _____

    _____

4. How might you get a holiday?

    _____

    _____

5. What are the steps to adjust a holiday?

    _____

    _____

6. How might you get a heavy weave or slice?

    _____

    _____

7. What are the steps to adjust a heavy weave or slice?

    _____

    _____

8. How might you get a hot spot or bleeding?

    _____

    _____

9. What are the steps to adjust a hot spot or bleeding?

    _____

    _____

10. What can you do to prevent flaws in the future?

    _____

    _____

# Learning Review

Read

With each technique, identify what you will focus on to improve your skills.

Reflect

What are some important new skills you have learned? What will you implement in your guest services?

Review

View the DVD and skill cards for each technique and what you need to improve.

Select/Prioritize

Identify the sectioning and foil steps that you need to practice on a doll head. Review your skill cards as you perform the technique.

Draw

On a head sheet, diagram each technique. Then windowpane the steps for slicing and weaving.

Share/Act

Teach what you have learned to a friend or coworker.

The Color System

PAUL MITCHELL
schools

Chapter 6
Color Play

Robert Cromeans

Stephanie Kocielski

Linda Yodice

Lucie Doughty

Audra Turner

Kate Caussey

Color Activities

How to Use the Interactive Color Map

Color Play

In hair coloring, there are rules to learn and guidelines to follow. Most of the content in this book has been focused on step-by-step sectioning, diagramming, numbers, and formulation, which mostly involve the "left brain." All of this information is valuable and necessary to become a successful hair colorist, as it will help you learn to be consistent. But what about the "right brain" or creative side?

Left Brain
- Analytical
- Numbers
- Engineering
- Technical

Right Brain
- Creative
- Emotions
- Color
- Art
- Music

The beauty of coloring hair is that it involves both sides of the brain. The first five chapters of this book fed the left side of your brain with so much information that it's time to feed the right side of your brain. This chapter is designed to not only stimulate your right brain, but to create balance in your learning as well. Enjoy!

 Activity

Read and answer the following questions to discover who or what inspires you as a colorist.

What are your favorite quotes about color, style, design, art, or creativity?

_____
_____
_____

What inspires you?

_____
_____
_____

What does color mean to you?

_____
_____

How does color express your creativity?

_____
_____

Which artists inspire you? Why?

_____
_____

Where do you find your creativity?

_____
_____

Where do you find inspiration?

_____
_____

Who are your mentors? Why?

_____
_____

Robert Cromeans
John Paul Mitchell Systems Global Artistic Director

■ **What are your favorite quotes about color, style, design, art, or creativity?**
My favorite quote I ever heard was, "You date your haircutter, but you marry your colorist!"

■ **What inspires you?**
Impossible things!

■ **What does color mean to you?**
Color says what you can't think of saying out loud!

■ **How does color express your creativity?**
It's 80 percent practicality and 20 percent creativity.

■ **Which artist(s) inspire you? Why?**
Salvador Dali because he said his mustache was like an antenna that received messages that others didn't seem to get. I feel my goatee is that receptor for me.

■ **Who are your mentors? Why?**
Every hairdresser who has the courage to pick up a tint brush!

Activity: Mystery Color

1) Give a learning partner three pieces of paper cut into 4x4-inch squares.

2) Ask him or her to cut the squares into any three shapes he or she would like, such as stars, waves, triangles, circles, squares, etc.

3) On a head sheet, design and diagram a creative Block Color technique using one or all shapes. Identify placement, effect, possible color choices, formulation, and which type of haircut would this Block Color technique best complement.

4) If possible, create the Block Color technique on a doll head. Take before and after pictures to help you learn.

5) Share with your learning partner the following:
   * *What did you learn or discover?*
   * *How would you do it differently next time?*
   * *Did the shapes fit the haircut?*
   * *Are you happy with the final results? Why or why not?*
   * *What was the overall effect?*

Stephanie Kocielski

Artistic Director for Paul Mitchell

■ **What inspires you?**
People, places, things, movements, daring to be different.

■ **What does color mean to you?**
A tool to change the way people feel about themselves, like a magic power to add a smile to you and your guest.

■ **How does color express your creativity?**
[It] adds to the movement of a haircut and defines the guest's individual look.

■ **Which artist(s) inspire you? Why?**
Dali; he is "out of the box" and melted things he didn't like…He thought differently than any other artist, stood out, and never grew up. The world knew him because he made a big deal about what he did…he dressed for success and talked it up. I think he was a closet hairdresser—look at the stash! Also, he sold his paintings for a lot of money because of the frame for the art and the entire package…He made sure business was involved, too.

■ **Where do you find your creativity?**
As soon as the guests put their faith in me and sit in the chair, the show starts. We need to go beyond what they feel and think of themselves and color is the most legal drug I can sell. It changes moods, makes people remember how they felt when they were happy, and gives them a new perspective of who they can become.

■ **Where do you find inspiration?**
Everywhere—just keep your eyes open; also look at old television shows in black and white and then watch color television to see how much tone, vibrancy, is there. Just one watch of *The Wizard of Oz* and I have to go to The Color Bar.

■ **Who are your mentors? Why?**
Jeanne Braa; she liked things simple and, as a hairdresser, she wanted it fast and focused. She made me really know about lightening hair, staying focused in the application, and how to make an area of hair stand out with color. Sam Lapin, a great man who invented modern color. Working with him made me understand how things worked. My kindergarten art teacher, as she never complained when I painted the kids' hair instead of paper.

Activity: Movie Night

The following movies are great examples of how color and light are used to help tell a story:

- *The Wizard of Oz*
- *Gone With the Wind*
- *What Dreams May Come*
- *Vertigo*
- *Singin' in the Rain*
- *Life Is Beautiful*
- *Charlie and the Chocolate Factory* (Tim Burton version)
- *Amélie*
- *Moulin Rouge!*
- *Edward Scissorhands*
- *Pee-wee's Big Adventure*

As you are enjoying any of these movies, answer the following questions:

1) How is color used to support the plot?

2) How is light used to support the story?

3) Which colors are used? Are they strong or muted colors?

4) Which emotions, mood, or feelings do the colors create?

5) How is light used in the movie?

6) Which emotions, mood, or feelings does the light create?

7) What message are the color and light trying to express?

8) Which colors express the following emotions?

Happiness_____	Anger _____
Love_____	Sadness _____
Joy_____	Envy _____
Passion_____	Loneliness _____

9) What else did you discover about color and light when watching the movie?

10) How did the movie spark your imagination?

Linda Yodice

Artistic Director for Paul Mitchell Professional Hair Color

■ **What are your favorite quotes about color, style, design, art, and creativity?**
"Abandoned restraint."

■ **What inspires you?**
Fashion: how it reflects past, present, and future.

■ **What does color mean to you?**
Visual proof of emotion and passion.

■ **How does color express your creativity?**
In hair, dimensional coloring helps me create texture, movement, and balance to a cut.

■ **Which artists inspire you?**
Pablo Picasso . . . Cubism
Paul Gauguin . . . color patterning
Vincent van Gogh . . . broad brush strokes
Claude Monet . . . play of light
Jackson Pollock . . . emotional abstraction
Leonardo da Vinci . . . master of art and science

■ **Where do you find your creativity?**
In arrangement; I like to move things around, change the order, see what happens when you take things out of balance. I love asymmetry . . . things slightly off balance.

■ **Where do you find inspiration?**
Mother Nature; she provides for us something different every day and teaches us about the past, present, and future.

■ **Who are your mentors?**

Mentors from afar:
• Frank Lloyd Wright spent a lifetime mastering the space in which we live.
• Einstein spent a lifetime mastering outer space.
• Dr. Wayne Dyer helps us master our inner space.

Mentors near:
John Paul Mitchell Systems artistic directors; we share something in common.

Activity: Match Game

1) Find some quiet time when you can identify color by looking at pictures in magazines; or go to a hardware store and load up on paint-chip samples; or gather some flowers, leaves, or stems from a garden.

2) Using **the color** swatch book, match the levels and tones of the colors you see in the pictures, paint chips, or garden. To achieve a perfect match, you may need to combine color swatches. For example, a picture of a mahogany table in a magazine could be a combination of 4NN and 4R in the swatch book. See how many different colors you can match and formulate.

3) Answer these questions:
   - *What did you learn?*
   - *Was this activity easy or difficult for you? Why or why not?*
   - *What else can you play this match game with?*

Lucie Doughty

Paul Mitchell Editorial Director

■ *How does color express your creativity?*
Color is such a great accessory; it can be changed often and there are a wide range of options. I love the color box we have at Paul Mitchell. It really is like an artist paint box. I love the bright colors of INKWORKS, but also enjoy the subtleties you can achieve with PM SHINES and **the color**.

■ *Which artists inspire you? Why?*
Gustav Klimt; the use of color, patterns, and detail in his work is so amazing to look at. There is a depth and emotion that draws you into all his work. I took a trip to Vienna, Austria, to see his paintings. It was an amazing experience to see his work so close. I also love contemporary art, Art Nouveau, and Expressionism.

■ *Where do you find inspiration?*
Where I live and the people around me; I love the sunshine and the ocean. I have developed great working relationships with the models I use for shoots. Many times, I'll imagine a hairstyle and think of which of the girls it will look great on. I absolutely pore over fashion magazines. I love the more obscure magazines that push the limits of hair and fashion.

Activity: Color Copy

1) Find a photo from a fashion magazine that shows dimensional hair color.
2) On a head sheet, diagram the color that you see in the photo.
3) Create the same technique on a doll head to see how closely you can come to duplicating the picture.
4) Take before and after pictures.
5) On a poster, assemble and glue the magazine picture, head sheet, color formulation, answers to the following questions, and before and after pictures of the doll head.
6) Present everything to your learning partner or the class.
7) Answer these questions:
   • *What was the placement? What technique was used?*
   • *What colors from **the color** swatch book match the colors you see?*
   • *What formulations would you use to achieve the same color result?*
   • *What type of haircut do you think the color was completed on?*
   • *What did you discover? What would you do differently?*

Audra Turner

Paul Mitchell Advanced Academy Color Education Leader

■ **What does color mean to you?**
Color is the most amazing outlet. We get to be artists, but our canvas is a living being that walks around talking about our art, like our own personal tour guide.

■ **Where do you find your creativity?**
I am inspired creatively by my daughter Veronica. She refuses artistic rules and boundaries. Because of this, she is always living "out of the box." She has given me ideas that I would never think of on my own.

■ **Where do you find inspiration?**
I find inspiration everywhere, but I think nature is my favorite. Mother Nature seems to do color combinations better than anyone.

■ **Who are your mentors? Why?**
I really love many artists, but children's sketches always put a smile on my face. They are honest because children draw things as they see them.

 ## Activity: Child's Play

1) Ask a child between the ages of 4 and 7 to draw a picture using crayons on 11x17-inch paper.
2) Discuss the drawing with the child: *What or who is in the picture? What are your favorite shapes? What are your favorite colors? What does the picture mean? What do the colors mean? Why did you use them? How does this picture make you feel? What sparks your imagination?*
3) Display the picture somewhere in your home, so that you see it for the next 30 days. Look at the picture often and ask yourself these questions:
   • *What do I love about this picture?*
   • *How does it make me feel?*
   • *How does this picture inspire me to be a better colorist? A better person?*
   • *What valuable lesson did I learn about color? About myself?*
   • *What sparks my imagination?*
   • *Which shapes and colors do I like?*
4) After 30 days, sit down with a box of crayons to draw and color a picture. Try to answer the questions through your drawing.
5) Share your drawing with a child.

Kate Caussey

Paul Mitchell Advanced Academy Lead Color Specialist

■ **What are your favorite quotes about color, style, design, art, and creativity?**

"Colors, like features, follow the changes of the emotions."
~ **Pablo Picasso** [Spanish painter and sculptor, 1881–1973]

"Color possesses me. I don't have to pursue it. It will possess me always, I know it."
~ **Paul Klee** [Swiss artist, 1879–1940]

"The purest and most thoughtful minds are those which love colour the most."
~ **John Ruskin** [British art critic and author, 1819–1900]

■ **What inspires you?**
My mood, fabrics, textures, and food.

■ **What does color mean to you?**
"Color is a basic human need . . . like fire and water, a raw material, indispensable to life."

■ **Which artists inspire you? Why?**

• Salvador Dali; he painted his dreams to make them a reality.

• Henri Matisse; he was an artist, sculptor, teacher, and lawyer. He thought he was a lawyer until he discovered he was an artist.

• M.C. Escher; he created visual illusions.

■ **Who are your mentors? Why?**

My mom; she taught me color theory when I was three; I just didn't realize it until I was 20.

Activity: Art Discovery

1) Look through art books or go to a museum. Find paintings that appeal to you and spend time studying them.

2) Study these elements of art to discover:

- Line — *What lines do you see?*

- Shape — *What shapes do you see?*
Two-dimensional
Flat
Height and width

- Form — *What forms do you see?*
Three-dimensional
Height, width, and depth

- Space — *What space do you see?*
Positive space
Negative space
Balance

- Texture — *What textures do you see?*
Smooth
Rough

- Value — *What values do you see?*
Light to dark
Dark to light

- Color — *What colors do you see?*
Warm — inviting, soothing, happy
Cool — disturbing, sad, hollow

3) Study these principles of art to discover:
   - Balance
   - Imbalance
   - Rhythm
   - Emphasis
   - Unity
   - Direction
   - Opacity
   - Transparency

4) Describe the painting. Describe all aspects including figures, animals, buildings, etc.

5) Describe and identify the elements of the painting.

6) Describe and identify the principles of the painting.

7) Analyze the elements and principles as organized by the artist. Describe how the artist manipulates them.

8) Interpret the painting, which means the expressive qualities of the painting, such as mood, feelings, statements, and emotions.

9) How does the painting inspire you as a hair colorist?

10) What did you learn about yourself as an artist? As a hair colorist?

11) Using inspiration from the art you chose, design and diagram a Block Color technique on a head sheet.

12) Consider the shapes and colors.

13) What type of haircut would your design be best suited for: one-length, layered, or graduated?

14) On a doll head, create the Block Color you designed. Take "before" and "after" pictures.

15) Share what you learned with a learning partner or the class.

Activity: Nature Color

Here is a fun activity to do in the spring or fall when the colors of nature are at their best and brightest.

1) Go outside.

2) Use an environmentally friendly bag and gather a variety of colorful spring flowers or fall leaves. Remember to be respectful of nature and personal property.

3) Using the flora you gathered and glue, colored markers or paints, and a sturdy poster board, create a color map.

4) You can also create Mother Nature's version of a color swatch book.

5) See if you can gather enough of the same color to create Levels 1–10. For example, can you gather red leaves ranging from Levels 1–10?

6) Create a dominant pigment chart.

7) See if you can find the following in nature:
   - Warm tones
   - Cool tones
   - Combination tones, such as red/brown, red/orange, red/violet, gold/brown, blue/violet

8) Answer these questions:
   - *What did you learn about nature?*
   - *What did you learn about levels and tones?*
   - *What colors did you discover that you didn't realize existed in nature?*
   - *How did this activity help you expand your knowledge of color?*
   - *How will you view colors in nature differently?*
   - *How does nature inspire you as a colorist?*
   - *What was the most valuable aspect you learned?*

9) Using inspiration from the colors in nature, design and diagram a Block Color technique on a head sheet.

10) Consider the shapes and colors.

11) What type of haircut would your design be best suited for: one-length, layered, or graduated?

12) On a doll head, create the Block Color you designed. Take "before" and "after" pictures.

13) Share what you learned with a learning partner or the class.

Watch and listen to "The Color System Trailer" on Disc One to answer the following questions.

1. What is Robert's goal for the industry? _____
   _____

2. How will The Color System help make that happen? _____
   _____

3. What three things does Lucie attribute her success to? _____
   _____

4. Which fundamental skills do you need to soar as a colorist? _____
   _____

5. In what ways does *The Color System* DVD address Multiple Intelligences?
   _____
   _____

6. Linda shares two areas in which we need to be more confident in our work. What are they?
   _____
   _____

7. What does Linda feel this DVD will do for you as a colorist?
   _____
   _____

8. How long has Robert been in this industry? What is the value of a seasoned stylist using this system? _____
   _____

9. As a salon owner, what does Robert look for when hiring? _____
   _____
   _____

10. What guarantee does Lucie share? _____
    _____

Color Word Search

```
S  L  P  Q  H  W  V  V  S  H  D  U  G  O  S
D  E  C  J  O  K  F  N  K  E  R  I  C  S  K
O  N  E  H  R  R  F  S  L  C  C  C  R  R  L
H  A  G  N  I  D  E  E  L  B  I  T  O  G  D
O  P  A  L  Z  B  L  A  G  P  L  W  I  E  W
L  L  I  A  O  G  P  A  I  N  L  G  N  O  E
I  G  U  C  N  F  V  T  N  I  I  S  S  C  N
D  C  J  I  T  K  A  D  O  O  I  V  I  W  L
A  F  U  T  A  L  X  F  R  T  G  L  A  X  W
Y  N  P  R  L  D  K  J  Y  U  S  A  N  E  R
M  U  S  E  H  O  T  S  P  O  T  T  I  M  W
I  V  J  V  G  N  I  K  C  O  L  B  T  D  C
C  R  O  W  N  V  W  V  T  Q  K  M  C  V  K
G  A  W  E  M  O  S  Q  I  S  G  A  L  V  S
J  I  T  R  Y  S  M  X  A  I  H  Y  Y  U  O
```

Bleeding	Slice	Panel	Locking
Diagonal	Crown	Vertical	Section
Horizontal	Foil Work	Density	Weaving
Occipital	Hot Spot	Holiday	

Color Glossary Words

Across

4. Refers to tones with blue to blue-violet bases
5. Dramatic change in color you want to be noticed and seen
6. Combination of porosity, elasticity, and texture
7. Spots missed on the hair or scalp due to poor product application
10. Section that creates a more diffused effect or sheet of color
11. To blend two or more substances
12. Strong effect, strands, and bands
13. The warmth or coolness of a color
14. Smaller workable area within a panel or segment
15. Noticeable change in color, as if you have someone's attention
16. A smaller area within a segment
17. Fine ribbons of hair colored within a section
21. Ability of hair to absorb or hold moisture
24. Sliver of hair within a section
25. The feel of a surface or fabric based on its diameter
26. Colors that contain the qualities of heat

Down

1. Ball of hair created by twisting it on top of itself
2. Degree of compactness of a substance
3. Small bony protrusion at the base of the skull
8. Residual melanin that will remain in the hair
9. To counterbalance an action or influence of color
18. Highest point at the top of the skull
19. Seepage of color or lightener from the foil
20. Section that gives a stronger effect, resulting in a wall or block of color
22. A soft, subtle color result; colors used within the same family of color
23. Back of the head just below the apex

Activity

View the DVD, click on the icon, and fill in the term and definition in the space below.

 Words to Remember

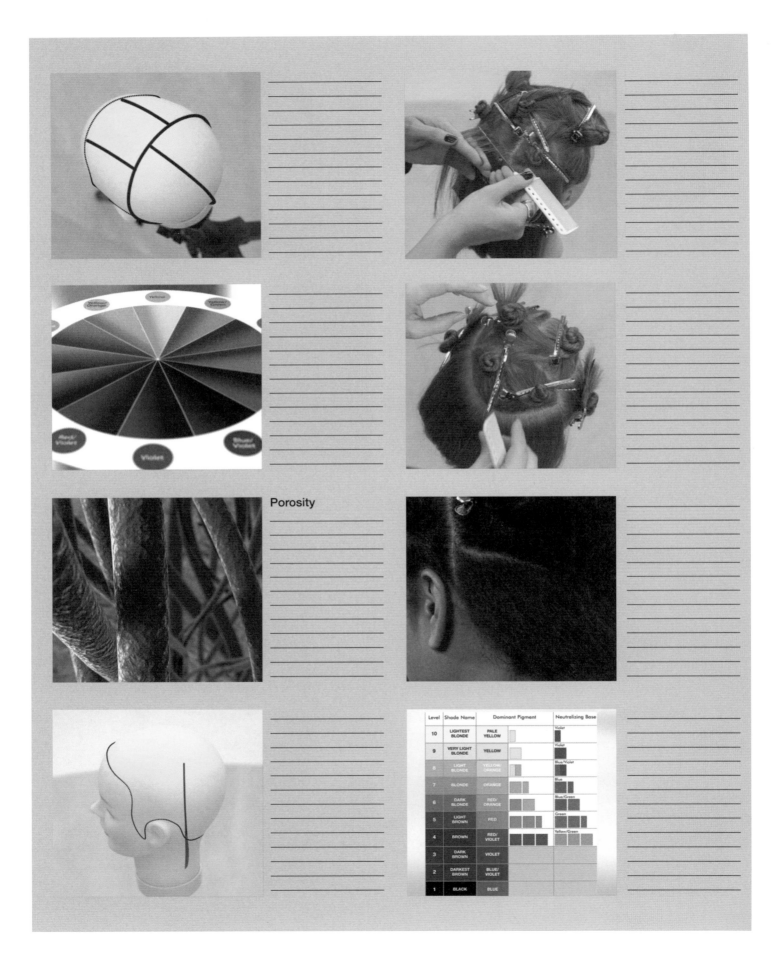

Porosity

Level	Shade Name	Dominant Pigment	Neutralizing Base
10	LIGHTEST BLONDE	PALE YELLOW	Violet
9	VERY LIGHT BLONDE	YELLOW	Violet
8	LIGHT BLONDE	YELLOW/ORANGE	Blue/Violet
7	BLONDE	ORANGE	Blue
6	DARK BLONDE	RED/ORANGE	Blue/Green
5	LIGHT BROWN	RED	Green
4	BROWN	RED/VIOLET	Yellow/Green
3	DARK BROWN	VIOLET	
2	DARKEST BROWN	BLUE/VIOLET	
1	BLACK	BLUE	

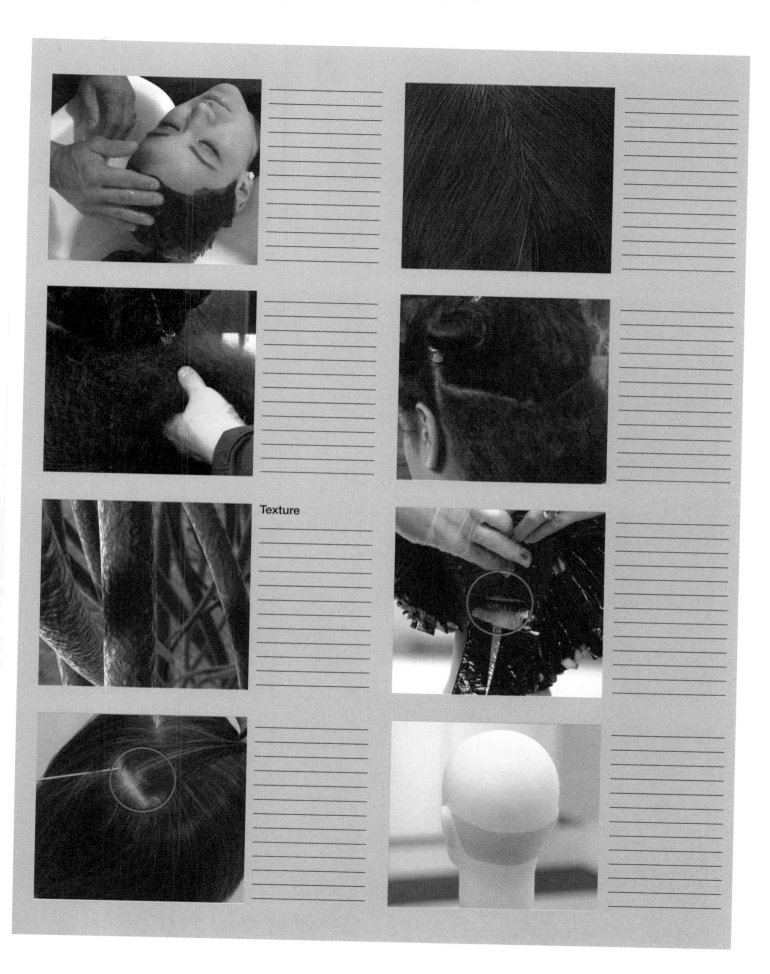

Texture

How to Use the Interactive Color Map

The Interactive Color Map is a tool designed to help you understand color theory and formulation based on the laws of color utilizing the Paul Mitchell **the color** Map.

Follow these directions to open the Interactive Color Map. Note: Clicking on the Interactive Color Map icon within the menu will only show a picture of the color map and does not open it.

Mac directions:
1. Insert Disc Two.
2. When the DVD begins, press Escape.
3. A DVD icon should appear on your screen; click to open.
4. Click to open the Mac file.
5. Double click on the Flash icon. The Interactive Color Map should open.
6. Play, learn, and enjoy!

PC directions:
1. Insert Disc Two.
2. When the DVD begins, press Escape.
3. Go to the Start menu, click on My Computer.
4. Go to the disc icon and right click; then click on Open.
5. Double click on the Interactive Color Map file.
6. Double click on the Windows file.
7. Double click on the Flash icon. The Interactive Color Map should open.
8. Play, learn, and enjoy!

Now that you have opened the Interactive Color Map, let's explain each piece, starting from the outside of the map then moving to the center.

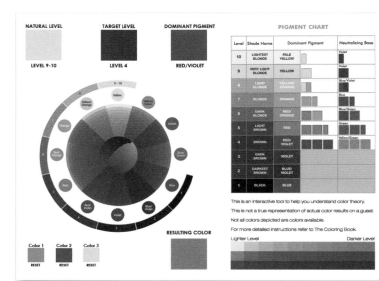

■ The outer ring or "C shape" represents Levels 1–10, which correspond to the levels in hair: 1 is the darkest level and 10 is the lightest level.

■ The colored dots within the outer ring or "C shape" represent dominant pigment, which is the color of natural pigment exposed at each level when lightening hair.

■ The color wheel itself represents your color choices and includes the "naturals and neutral beiges" within the center.

■ You will note a gradation of color moving from light to dark within the wheel. The lightest gradient or "ring" on the outside represents a Level 10 at that tone. The darkest gradient or "ring" on the inside of the wheel represents a Level 1 at that tone.

■ The rings represent the target colors you can select from.

■ The pigment chart to the right has been added as a reference for your use.

Let's look at the boxes.

■ The top-left box represents the natural level (or canvas level).

■ The top-center box represents the target level.

■ The top-right box represents the dominant pigment at the target level you selected.

■ The three bottom boxes titled Color 1, Color 2, and Color 3 represent the target color(s) you select. You can select (or mix) one, two, or three target colors depending on whether you want to neutralize, intensify, or enhance the result.

■ The bottom-right box titled Resulting Color shows the final result or the combination of levels and tones you selected.

Natural Level (box) + Target Level (box) + Color 1, Color 2, and Color 3 (boxes) = Resulting Color (box)

Tools needed:

1. Formulation worksheet (blank) and a pen

2. Steps to formulation, located in The Color System skill cards or *The Coloring Book*

Let's walk through an example to help you become familiar with how to use the Interactive Color Map.

1. Click once on the Natural Level box.

2. Select a natural level from the outer ring or "C shape" by clicking once on the level you desire. For example, click on Level 5.

3. Click once on the Target Level box.

4. Select a target level by clicking on the outer ring or "C shape." For example, click on Level 8. The dominant pigment at the target level you selected will automatically appear in the Dominant Pigment box and in the Result box. For example, the dominant pigment at a Level 8 will be yellow/orange.

5. Decide the tonal end result. For example, this service guest wants to neutralize the yellow/orange dominant pigment.

6. Click once on the Color 1 box at the bottom of the screen. Click on the tone at the target level that will neutralize the dominant pigment. For example, click on a blue/violet tone at a Level 8. The target level (8) and target color (blue/violet) neutralize the dominant pigment (yellow/orange) and the final result will appear in the Resulting Color box.

Now, try this. Let's pretend that The Color Bar has run out of blue/violet tone at a Level 8. As a result, you will need to combine other colors to neutralize the yellow/orange dominant pigment.

7. Click on the Reset button to clear the Color 1 box.

8. To make blue/violet, click on the Color 1 box and select the blue tone at a Level 8; then click on the Color 2 box and select the blue tone at a Level 8; click on the Color 3 box and select the red tone at a Level 8. Combining two parts blue and one part red equals blue/violet and the final result will appear in the Resulting Color box.

Congratulations: You are now ready to play with, learn, and enjoy the Interactive Color Map!

Activity

Play with the Interactive Color Map to complete the following color activities. Remember, there can be more than one way to achieve the same result.

❶ Canvas level 6
❷ Target level 4
❸ What is the dominant pigment?
❹ You want to enhance the color. What are your choices?
❺ What differences do you see in the results?

_____
_____
_____
_____
_____

❶ Canvas level 8
❷ Target level 6
❸ What is the dominant pigment?
❹ You want to intensify the color. What are your choices?
❺ What differences do you see in the results?

_____
_____
_____
_____
_____

❶ Canvas level 5
❷ Target level 7
❸ Your service guest wants to be a rich, vibrant red.
❹ What is the dominant pigment?
❺ What would your selection be? You can select up to three colors.

_____
_____
_____
_____
_____

❶ Canvas level 8
❷ Target level 10
❸ Your service guest wants to be a strawberry blonde.
❹ What is the dominant pigment?
❺ What would your selection be? You can select up to three colors.
❻ What differences do you see in the results?

_____
_____
_____
_____
_____

❶ Canvas level 7
❷ Target level 5; enhanced
❸ What is the dominant pigment?
❹ What would your selection be? You can select up to three colors.
❺ What differences do you see in the results?

_____
_____
_____
_____
_____

❶ Canvas level 2
❷ Target level 3
❸ Your service guest wants to be a bright, vibrant red.
❹ What is the dominant pigment?
❺ What would your selection be? You can select up to three colors.
❻ What differences do you see in the results?

_____
_____
_____
_____
_____

❶ Canvas level 5

❷ Target level 7

❸ Your service guest wants to be a neutral blonde.

❹ What is the dominant pigment?

❺ What would your selection be?

❻ You can only use primary colors. What would your selection be?

_____
_____
_____
_____
_____

❶ Canvas level 4 red, previously colored

❷ Target level 4, no red

❸ What is the dominant pigment?

❹ What is the result if you apply yellow/green?

❺ What is the result if you apply yellow/orange?

❻ What is the result if you apply a NN?

_____
_____
_____
_____
_____

The Color System

PAUL MITCHELL schools

Color Tools

Color Wheel

Formulation Worksheet

Head Sheets

Windowpane

Paul Mitchell Advanced Education

Color Wheel

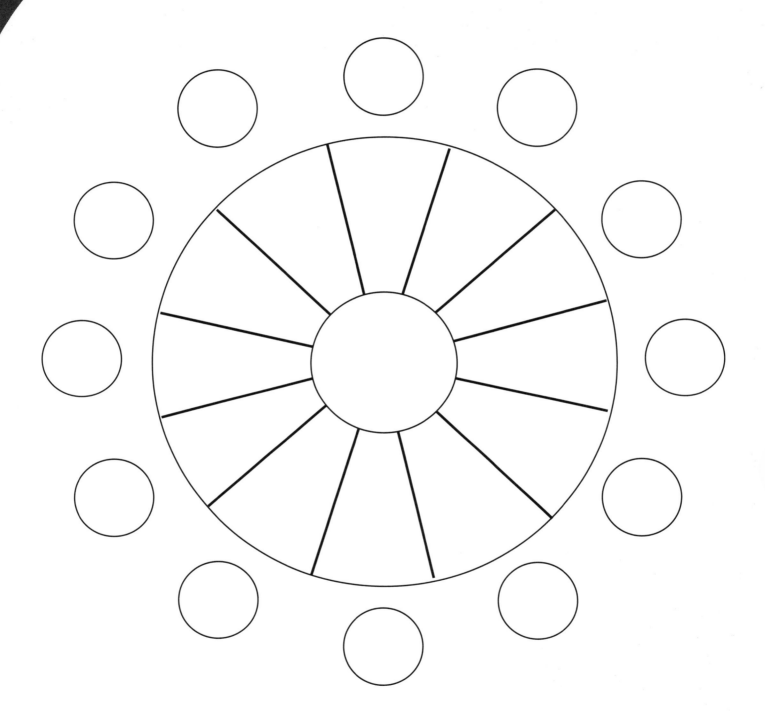

Formulation Worksheet

PAUL MITCHELL®
PROFESSIONAL HAIR COLOR

Formulation Worksheet

Natural Level _____

Canvas Level _____

Desired Level _____

Dominant Pigment
  at Desired Level _____

Desired Tonal Result _____

Pre-Post-Treatment Products Used:

_____

_____

Formula(s) Used/Developer(s) Used:

Formula 1 _____

Formula 2 _____

Formula 3 _____

Fabric:

Elasticity _____

Porosity _____

Texture _____

Final Score _____

Repigmentation Formula _____

_____

Timing _____

_____

PAUL MITCHELL®
PROFESSIONAL HAIR COLOR

Formulation Worksheet

Natural Level _____

Canvas Level _____

Desired Level _____

Dominant Pigment
  at Desired Level _____

Desired Tonal Result _____

Pre-Post-Treatment Products Used:

_____

_____

Formula(s) Used/Developer(s) Used:

Formula 1 _____

Formula 2 _____

Formula 3 _____

Fabric:

Elasticity _____

Porosity _____

Texture _____

Final Score _____

Repigmentation Formula _____

_____

Timing _____

_____

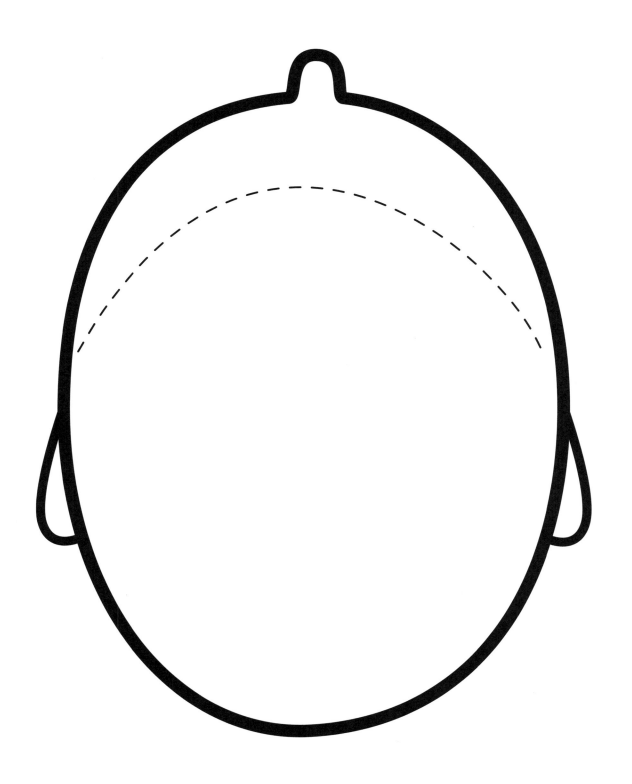

Windowpane

Topic: _____

Paul Mitchell Advanced Education

Would you like to experience these color techniques in a hands-on class? We offer three-day color classes.

Core Color — Learn the rules! Gain a true understanding of hair color. Experience integral hair color placements featured in the Paul Mitchell Color System. Ignite your passion and confidence for creating beautiful hair color.

Adaptive Color — Apply the rules! Take the rules you mastered in Core Color and apply them to adapt your color knowledge. Feel confident to step out of the box and explore your creativity by combining placement and technique.

For course descriptions, tuition costs, hotel, and travel information, contact the Advanced Academy at (877) 903-5375 ext. 1507; or enroll online at www.PaulMitchell.edu or e-mail AdvancedAcademy@PaulMitchell.edu.

Glossary

Becoming a successful hair colorist requires fluency in the language of hair coloring, which you will find in this glossary of terms and the learning terms and tools.

Acid A chemical substance with a pH lower than 7.0, including any substance whose molecules release hydrogen ions in water. Acids have a sour taste, turn blue litmus paper red, and unite with bases to form salts.

Alkali A chemical compound with a pH higher than 7.0. A class of compounds that react with acid to form salts, turn red litmus paper blue, and react with fats to form soap.

Amino Acids Compound molecules that link to create polypeptides and are commonly referred to as the "building blocks" of protein.

Ammonia A colorless, pungent gas. When mixed with hydrogen peroxide, activates the oxidation process on melanin and allows the melanin to decolorize; swells the hair cuticle.

Apex The highest point at the top of the skull. The apex can be located by laying the comb flat on the top of the head; the point where the comb rocks back and forth is the apex.

Ash In hair coloring, a color or tonal quality having no colors that reflect warmth. Blue, green, and violet are generally the base tones of ashen colors.

Base The combination of buffers, fragrances, stabilizers, and conditioning agents in which color pigments "live" within the tube or bottle; can also include ammonia.

Bleach See lightener.

Bleeding Seepage of color or lightener from a foil caused by too much product in the foil; applied product passed the fold of the foil or applied heat caused the foil to swell and product to leak out onto the hair (see holiday).

Block Color — All-over coverage with dimension using color (and sometimes lightener) within a combination of foil work using large panels. Block Color is customized to every haircut.

Canvas Level — See existing level and natural level.

Chevron Parting — In partings, two opposing diagonal angles that meet at a point and flow away from the other.

Color Balance — A mixture of a lightener product, hydrogen peroxide, and shampoo, usually mixed in equal parts. Used professionally to remove small quantities of artificial and natural pigment from the hair; not as aggressive as full-strength bleach.

Color Correction — Color correction occurs anytime artificially colored or lightened hair is made lighter or darker. Thorough consultation and strand tests are recommended.

Color Pigment — The natural coloring matter or substance that lives in a base (see base, direct dye, and indirect dye).

Contributing Pigment — Pigment that remains in the hair and is exposed when the natural color is lightened. Contributing pigment must be taken into consideration when formulating hair color.

Cool — In hair coloring, any tones not containing warmth. Generally refers to tonal qualities with blue to blue-violet bases.

Corrective Base — Colors that are opposite on **the color** Map. Combined together at the same level, the two neutralize each other, making a tone neither warm nor cool.

Cortex — The second and most substantial layer of the hair strand. The cortex contains nearly all of the melanin of the hair and is also the source of its strength and elasticity.

Crown — The area on the back of the skull just below the apex.

Cuticle — The translucent protein outer layer of the hair fiber.

Decolorize — The action of removing artificial and/or natural pigment from the hair, generally using a mixture of bleach (alkali) and hydrogen peroxide (acid).

Demi-permanent Hair Color — A no-lift, deposit-only oxidation hair color that generally gives more gray blending than semi-permanent colors. May have both direct and indirect pigments and can leave a slight line of demarcation; requires a developer.

Density — The degree of compactness of a substance; the amount per designated area, such as the amount of hair per square inch.

Deposit	In hair coloring, the action of placing dye intermediates into the hair shaft.
Developer	An oxidizing agent, such as hydrogen peroxide (H_2O_2), that provides the necessary oxygen to develop color molecules and create a change in color.
Diagonal Placement	A diagonal section that creates a more diffused effect or sheet of color since the hair falls from different points; works well with graduation.
Dimensional Color	Color placement containing more than one color that creates dimension and movement within the shape (see also Block Color).
Direct Dye or Direct Pigment	Large pre-developed color molecules that deposit into the hair primarily between the cuticle and cortex layers; does not always require oxidation to develop or color the hair.
Dominant Pigment	See contributing pigment.
Dye Intermediate	An organic compound that develops into color after reacting with a developer (hydrogen peroxide).
Elasticity	The ability of the hair to stretch and return to its normal shape.
Emulsify	To blend two or more substances; to make into a fine dispersion of minute droplets of one liquid in another in which it is not soluble or miscible.
Energy	The fundamental active entity of the universe; the ability to do work. Energy cannot be created or destroyed, but only converted from one form to another. For example, hydrogen peroxide or H_2O_2 is "energy"; the higher the volume (10, 20, 30, or 40 volume of H_2O_2) of developer mixed with color or lightener, the more energy (oxidation of artificial pigment and/or decolorization of natural pigment) converted.
Enhance	To increase or warm up what is naturally in the hair by using either an N or warmer tone, such as gold or WB (see talk in "Whisper, Talk, Shout").
Enzyme	A protein catalyst produced within a living organism that speeds up specific chemical reactions.
Existing Level	The level of how light or dark hair is naturally or artificially.
Fabric	The combination of porosity, elasticity, texture, and overall condition of the hair.
Fibril	A tiny filament or fiber found within the formation of cells.
Fluorescent Light	Light created by ultraviolet radiation from mercury vapor that is inexpensive to use and maintain, often used in large stores. Reduces shadows and spreads light more evenly; reducing shadows is important when cutting hair, but this lighting is inappropriate for color evaluation. Fluorescent lighting accents all cool tones in the hair and skin with unpleasant results.

Formation	Structure or arrangement; the formation of hair can be straight, wavy, curly, or extra curly.
Frontal Bone	The frontal bone is also known as the forehead.
Gray Blending	Coloring gray hair and allowing some of the gray to continue to show, creating a blended effect.
Gray Coverage	Coloring hair and completely covering the gray.
Highlift Hair Color	Permanent hair color formulated to provide the most lift and control with deposit of warmth in a single process on virgin hair.
Highlighting	Coloring hair strands lighter than the natural hair color.
Holiday	Can have a double meaning: 1) a euphemism for bright spots or streaks at the scalp area when foils bleed (see bleeding); or 2) a spot missed on the hair or scalp due to a poor application of product.
Horizontal Diagonal Back	An angle between the horizontal and diagonal with a movement flowing toward the back of the head. To locate: find the horizontal angle, find the diagonal angle, and go midway between the two to reach the horizontal diagonal. Place the angle flowing toward the back of the head to locate the horizontal diagonal back.
Horizontal Placement	A horizontal section that gives a stronger effect resulting in a wall or block of color, falling to one point; more symmetrical; works well with one-length hair.
Hot Spot	See holiday and bleeding.
Hydrogen Peroxide	Also known as H_2O_2; an acid on the pH scale. It is a bleaching (lightening) and oxidizing (developing artificial pigment) agent; readily broken down into water and oxygen. In solid pure states, it is highly stable. In lower percentages, a stabilizer is added. Available in liquid or cream.
Incandescent Light	Light seen with regular light bulbs; favors warm tones such as red, pink, coral, and yellow. Commonly used in homes, skin care salons, and makeup areas. Known as warm lighting and gives a warm reflection on the hair while muting cooler tones, such as green, blue, gray, or aqua. This unbalanced color perception could be deceiving if used for color evaluation.
Indirect Dye or Indirect Pigment	A dye or pigment that must undergo oxidation to color hair. The aniline-derived dye intermediates of demi-permanent and permanent hair color are indirect dyes (see oxidative dye).
Intensify	To add more to what occurs naturally in the hair at the existing level; to choose tones that are near or the same as the dominant pigment tone at the target level (see shout in "Whisper, Talk, Shout").

Keratin	A tough, water-soluble protein found in the epidermis of the nails and hair.
Level	In hair coloring, the measure used for the lightness or darkness of hair color; for example, Level 1 is the darkest color or black and Level 9/10 is the lightest color or blonde.
Lift	The amount of lightening or bleaching action assigned to a chemical product.
Lighten	The action of removing color from the hair using a lightening or bleaching agent (see decolorize).
Lightener	An alkaline compound used to remove natural color and/or artificial pigments from the hair, or to decolorize. Lightener products are available in powder, cream, oil, and paste forms.
Line of Demarcation	An obvious difference between two colors or levels on the hair shaft.
Lock or Locking	A process of securing a foil so that it does not slip, used in specific areas such as the hairline, crown, or at the top of the head. Used in a weave only.
Lowlighting	Coloring hair strands darker than the natural or current hair color.
Mastoid Bone	The prominent bone behind the ear that projects from the temporal bone of the skull.
Mastoid Division Line	A vertical division line that extends from the apex down to the mastoid process on either side, separating the front segment from the back segment.
Mastoid Process	Two mastoid processes are present, located in the areas behind both ears; it is the posterior portion of the temporal bone and serves as a muscle attachment.
Medulla	The innermost layer of the hair strand, which is sometimes intermittent or even absent. The medulla may contain some melanin.
Melanin	Dark brown or black pigment granules found in the hair cortex that create natural hair color.
Metamerism	The play of light on color.
Milliliter (ml)	A unit of liquid measurement utilizing the metric system; one thousandth of a liter.
Nape	The area of the head from the occipital bone to the bottom hairline of the neck and extending to the hairlines on each side behind the ears.

Natural Color	The color of the hair as provided naturally, without chemical additives or the action of environmental or artificial effects.
Natural Level	The level of how light or dark hair is naturally.
Natural Recession	The front hairline at the parietal ridge.
Neutralize	To counterbalance an action or influence of color; to select a tone or color on **the color** Map opposite the dominant pigment tone or color at the target level (see whisper in "Whisper, Talk, Shout").
Non-oxidative or Non-oxidizing	The quality of substances that do not oxidize, or combine or become combined chemically with oxygen; in reference to color pigments that do not require oxidation (see direct dyes).
Occipital Bone	The small, bony protrusion at the base of the skull where the neck joins the skull. It can be felt by placing your hand at the back of the head and feeling the joining point between the skull and neck.
Opaque	Blocking light; not able to be seen through. Opaque hair color does not allow light to filter through the strands. Hair that is colored with an opaque product looks dense, solid, and heavily or uniformly colored. Contrast translucent.
Ounce (oz)	A unit of weight of one-sixteenth of a pound within the standard measuring system within the United States.
Oxidative Dye	A small intermediate dye that is colorless until mixed with hydrogen peroxide. It then develops and deposits into the cortex and, when combined with the dominant pigment, creates the final color result.
Oxidize	To combine with oxygen. When melanin is lightened with hydrogen peroxide, which is an oxidizer, it is oxidized, or combined with or broken apart by oxygen, resulting in a chemical change. When the artificial pigments of the oxidative hair color are mixed with hydrogen peroxide, they also are oxidized and chemically reformed.
Panel	A smaller area within a segment.
Parietal Bones	Two large, irregularly quadrilateral bones between the frontal and occipital bones that together form the sides and top of the skull.
Parietal Ridge	The area of the skull where the parietal bones of the head begin to curve. It is also the point at which completely straight hair begins to fall in a vertical direction.
Permanent Hair Color	Hair color products capable of coloring the natural pigment lighter (lift), darker (deposit), or producing tonal changes at the same level. Oxidative pigments that penetrate into the cortex; require a developer; leave a line of demarcation; and give 100 percent gray coverage.

pH	The chemical designation for potential hydrogen; a figure that represents the percentage of acid or alkali present in a solution.
Pigmentation	The deposit of pigment in the hair.
Porosity	The ability of the hair to absorb and/or hold moisture.
Potential Hydrogen	The relative degree of acidity and alkalinity of a substance.
Pre-lighten	The removal or decolorization of the natural and/or artificial pigments from the hair prior to the application of another chemical or product. The first step of a double-process service: first, lifting or lightening the hair, followed by the application of a toner or color.
Primary Colors	The pure or fundamental colors that cannot be achieved from mixing other colors. The three primary colors are red, yellow, and blue.
Pure White Light	Light ideal for color evaluation. If possible, high-intensity lighting should be supplied in the color area. The only true white light is the light supplied by the sun.
Repigment	The process of replacing the dominant pigment (warm tones) that has been removed in a lightening process.
Resistant Hair	Nonporous hair with a tight cuticle layer that slows or prohibits the entrance of moisture.
Saturation	The degree of color pigments available in a hair color product; also the amount of product placed on the hair.
Secondary Colors	The colors immediately derived from combining two primary colors. The three secondary colors are orange, violet, and green.
Section	A smaller, workable area within a panel or segment; when coloring or cutting a section, is generally ¼ inch or less in size. The hair that is to be sliced or weaved is known as a section.
Segment	The hair can be divided into four to five segments. More than five segments are known as panels.
Semi-permanent Hair Color	No-lift hair color that lasts approximately from haircut to haircut depending on the porosity of the hair. Mostly direct pigment, but can have some indirect pigment, requiring a developer; deposit-only giving a 30–50-percent gray blending.
Slice or Slicing	A sliver of hair within a section; the slicing technique creates an effect that is stronger than the weave because the result is more bold.

Strand Test	Used on artificially colored hair, a test given on a small section of hair before a color or lightening service to determine the color result, formulation, development time, the hair's ability to withstand chemicals, number of service visits needed for the desired end result, and the knowledge to say yes or no to performing the service.
Target Level	The finished level of the color desired.
Temple	The small areas just above and in front of the ears on each side of the head. They are pulse points for blood flow and flex points for the facial muscles. If you clench your teeth, you can feel the muscles flex below the skin of the temples.
Temporal Bones	A pair of compound bones forming the sides and base of the skull; supports the part of the face known as the temples.
Temporary Hair Color	A deposit-only hair color that generally lasts from shampoo to shampoo depending on the porosity of the hair. Temporary color is direct or non-oxidative pigment that does not require a developer.
Tertiary Colors	The third, or tertiary, colors derived from combining one primary color and one of the secondary colors next to it on **the color** Map. The six tertiary colors are red-violet, red-orange, yellow-orange, yellow-green, blue-green, and blue-violet.
Texture	The feel of a surface or fabric; the texture of hair can be fine, medium, or coarse, based on its diameter.
Tonal Bases	The predominant color visible within a hair color.
Tone	The warmth or coolness of a color.
Toner	The color to be used after pre-lightening; the second step of a double-process service.
Translucent	Permitting light to pass through. Translucent hair color allows light to diffuse through the strands and allows the eye to see "into" the hair, giving it a dimensional appearance; seeing both highlight and undertones. Contrast opaque.
Variations in Fiber	Overall differences in the condition and texture of the hair.
Vertical Placement	A vertical section that gives a strong effect resulting in strands and bands or stripes of color falling to one point; works well with layers.
Warm	A description of colors that contain the qualities of heat, or warm tones. Warm colors include red, yellow, orange, and gold.

Volume	A measurement of the degree of oxygen gas within a hydrogen peroxide solution; the amount of oxygen a given concentration of hydrogen peroxide (H_2O_2) will release. For example, 10-volume H_2O_2, which is the same as 3 percent, releases 10 times its volume in oxygen (one ounce of 10-volume H_2O_2 releases 10 ounces of oxygen); 20-volume H_2O_2 releases 20 times its volume (two ounces of 20-volume releases 40 ounces of oxygen).
Weave or Weaving	A technique used to create a softer, natural highlighted effect; fine ribbons of hair color within a section.
Working Volume	A reference to the volume strength of a combination of developer and color or developer and bleach. For example, a formula of one part color and one part 20-volume H_2O_2 has a working volume of 10. Mixing equal parts of color with developer dilutes the volume in half. This is why it is safe to put equal parts of 40-volume and color on the scalp because, in reality, you have a working volume of 20. However, a mixture of one part bleach and one part 20-volume has a working volume of 30. Mixing equal parts of bleach and developer increases the volume by 10. Therefore, equal parts of bleach and 10-volume becomes 20; 20-volume becomes 30; and 30-volume becomes 40. This is why it is not safe to put equal parts of 40-volume and bleach on the scalp because, in reality, you have a working volume of 50.
"Whisper, Talk, Shout"	Whisper — a soft, subtle color result; colors used within the same family of color; the effect of a whisper you can barely hear. Talk — a noticeable change in color, as if you have someone's attention. Shout — a dramatic change in color, you want to be noticed and heard.
Zulu Knot	Originating from southeast African Zulu tribes, a tight coil of hair created from twisting a hair section around itself into a ball that lies on the scalp.

Learning Terms and Tools

Descriptive/ Colorful Words
Words that create a strong visual impact for the learner or guest. It is beneficial to use descriptive/colorful words in your color consultations.

Dream Board
A visual picture or collage that represents one's goals, hopes, and visions.

Forward-focused Questions
Questions phrased in an open format using positive or neutral words that focus on solutions.

Learning Center
An area on the clinic floor, salon, or classroom that provides a self-directed learning activity, including visual, audio, or kinesthetic information. Learning centers are a great way to teach guests about products and Take Home.

Learning Map
A nonlinear visual representation on one or more topics to present information; outlines key ideas with main "arteries" or branches and smaller sub-points branching from them.

Multiple Intelligence (MI)
A learning theory based on the concept that we learn in unique ways within seven different intelligences, including verbal/linguistic, math/logic, spatial, body/kinesthetic, musical, interpersonal, and intrapersonal.

Windowpane
A nonlinear note-taking tool that illustrates main concepts in a grid using pictures and words.